MW00377639

First Acknowledgement goes to God for his Love and for making ways for me when I couldn't for myself. I read somewhere that Mans' main motivation to accomplish and achieve was in pursuit of a Lady's Love. Mom all these years later, it's still you. I love you; I love you; I love you. Thank you to my great niece Shayla for helping me put my manuscript together. Thank you, Uncle Joe, Cousin Luther, good friend Lucius Boddie and a host of other friends and family for your support even when you all didn't know what I was writing about.

Thank you to my 2 English Professors, Ms. Turner-Gaston and Mrs. Mitchell at Atlanta Metropolitan State College for the As' and empowering my belief that I could indeed write a book. Thanks to Dr. Ricardo A. Frazer for his book, Psychological Wellness and being proof with my very own eyes, that it could be done. Thank you, Dr. Baldwin, even though you didn't give me all As'. I learned so much about the Criminal Justice System and its' working from both sides.

Lastly, but certainly not the least, I acknowledge all the

famous people and those not so famous that I mentioned in book that have inspired me personally and so many others around the world.

I Love America But America Don't Love Me

Prologue

My memoirs and reflections are about systemic racism, and includes some history lessons exposing America's original terrorist, their tendencies, beliefs and the tools used so that blacks, whites, brown and red people can all recognize and eliminate the pitfalls of racism and cynicism, as we all pursue "Life," "Liberty" and "Happiness," ideals and principles for which America boasts. In my memoirs, I must call out America on some its fouls against African Americans, Native Americans, and others since my great-great-grandfather set foot on American soil as a slave. I have sincere hopes that we can work on our moral compasses and principles and try to love as a country, in hopes of attaining, in the words of George Clinton, "One Nation under a Groove." By no means am I a saint, merely a product of my environment and circumstances. In this book, you will find that I love America, but America don't love me. However, I still have sincere hopes of America becoming a great big melting pot of love, growing and glowing, like a bouquet of flowers, in the greatest country on Earth. If you look deep and believe in Adam and Eve, then you know that we're all related anyway. Accept

3

I Love America But America Don't Love Me

that fact, and we can all just FLOW and live up to the title, the

UNITED STATES of AMERICA.

In order to better understand my story, I think it's important
to know where I come from, to see how I went where I did, and
wound up here. I was born in Dawson, Georgia, a city in the
southwest, about 167 miles south of Atlanta, Georgia. Some notable
black folks from Dawson, who made it out, and found success
somewhere else, are Benjamin J. Davis, Jr., born in 1903. After
graduating from Harvard Law School, he became a member of the
City Council for the City of New York City in 1943, representing
Harlem. In 1951, he went to prison for five years because of his
pursuit for justice and equality. One of the highlights in his career
was his defense of Angelo Herndon, in the 1930s. Herndon was
arrested and jailed for the charge of "Insurgency" because he tried to
form a union to highlight Fair Labor standards. His conviction was
eventually overturned by the United States Supreme Court, with
Benjamin J. Davis at the helm.

Another Dawsonian was Walter Washington. Walter was
born in 1915. He went on to become the first black Mayor of
Washington, DC, our nation's capital. Otis Redding, who many

believed was born in Macon, Georgia, was in fact born in Dawson, in 1941. To this day, Dawson has not recognized and honored these native citizens. Each had to leave in order to GLOW and be recorded in the history books.

However, there is no mention at all in the history books about my father's maternal grandfather, my great grandfather, Eugene Armstrong. Eugene died a mysterious death in Baldwin County, Georgia at the age of 44, while in prison in 1931. There is no mention of the murder of Rufus Bridges and his wife after a group of KKK gathered and set fire to their residence in Terrell County, in 1952. Jesse Dukes, my uncle Luther's wife, Lois' brother, whose father was arrested and charged with the murder of his son and daughter-in-law spent over a year in jail before he was found not guilty of the crime in late 1953 by an all-White jury. As of today, this mystery has not been solved. However, rumor had it that Rufus was late plowing a field and his boss got upset about it.

There is no mention in the history books about Dawson, Georgia resident, James Brazier, a World War II Veteran. James fought for America and survived the war, but not the racism that was rampant in Dawson. He was abducted from his home in the spring of

1958 by Dawson police, on a Sunday evening. He was beat up and denied medical treatment. More than one local doctor passed him off as just being drunk, but the beating resulted in his death five days later.

On the day of the beating, he happened across his father who was also being beaten by Dawson police. It was said simply because they envied black men driving nice cars and having nice things. James Brazier had a brand new 1958 Chevrolet and he'd past his 1956 Chevrolet down to his father. His income was higher than the police and most of the white people in town because of his job at the Chevrolet dealership, two other jobs and income from the two jobs that his wife worked. James and his wife worked to meet their children's needs and tried to live the "American Dream."

Even on the day of James Brazier, Jr.'s funeral, racism wouldn't take the day off. James Brazier, Sr. was arrested again, for supposedly running a stop sign, while family members grieved at the church. His murder would have most likely gone unpunished if not for the dogged pursuit for justice by his widow, Hattie.

In the beginning, even the authorities in Macon, GA and FBI in Atlanta, turned a blind eye to his murder it seemed. But Mrs.

Brazier stayed on the case until a measure of justice was served.

There is quite a bit mentioned in the history books of the church bombing at the 16th Street Baptist Church in Birmingham, Alabama where four little Black Girls were killed in 1963. However, there is no mention in the history books of the five black church burnings in Dawson and Terrell County, Georgia during that same era.

Moving past the countless number of despicable acts against black folks murdered and missing in Dawson and the surrounding areas through 1979 when Dawson suffered another notable miscarriage of justice which resulted in, "The Dawson 5". In this case, five black men and boys were beaten and forced by police to confess to a murder of a white man by a white man. They were held captive for more than a year and a half before they were exonerated, with help from the City of Atlanta.

The maternal side of my family weathered the storm called racism and survived Dawson. However, I heard stories about weapons being strategically placed around their properties in Dawson to prevent family members from suffering the same fate as James Brazier. This is where I'm from.

I Love America But America Don't Love Me

Who I am? The first black blood for my branch of the

Crumbleys' came in 1860 when my great-great grandfather James J.

Crumbley impregnated one of his only two slaves, both females. One

of those females was my great-great grandmother, Catherine Harden,

she was only 15 years old at the time. Catherine was a mulatto, most

likely 3/4 white. In those times, my family described her as being

able to pass for white. No one knows where Catherine came from.

She was born in 1845 and mysteriously died in 1879 at the age of 34.

Albert Crumbley, James and Catherine's only son from that

union, was my great grandfather, who seems to have been loved by

his father. At the end of slavery, Albert and Catherine received

some land in GA, money and some mules from J. J. But the family

didn't hold on to the land after Albert passed away. After the family

sold the land, they moved to Florida and lived for about a year

before returning to Dawson to lease the same land. I've never

understood their thinking on this rationale.

The Indian Blood that runs in my veins is due to Albert

uniting with Hassie Green, the daughter of freed slave, Clark Green

and Mariah, a full-blooded Indian, born in Virginia. Mariah

somehow found her way to Georgia. Her family had most likely been kicked off one of the reservations in Virginia when European immigrants decided that they wanted the land. I have always wondered if her or her parents were victims of Andrew Jackson's, "Indian Removal Policy." The IRP forced Indians to track the most inhumane journey westward that would later be known as, "The Trail of Tears." This was a journey in which an estimated 4000 Native Americans died along the way. I read somewhere that the IRP was precipitated when gold was discovered on Indian land in Dahlonega, GA. And the European settlers acquired the land to clear for white settlement. Will the original terrorists please stand up? Mariah would eventually unite with Clark and they bore around eight children, including my Great Grandma Hassie.

Hassie and Albert's union produced several daughters and three sons, including Luther, my maternal grandfather Luther and his brother Uncle Albert whom were both instrumental in the lives of all the Crumbleys They were the strength and backbone that anchored the Crumbleys through the racist storms that existed during those times.

Luther united with Ophelia Pickett-Blackshear, the daughter of Henry Pickett and Corene Blackshear. Corene was the daughter

9

of Jane Oglesby and Albert Blackshear. Luther and Ophelia's' union produced six daughters and six sons, which includes the 4th child my Momma, whom I Love with All My Might!

My desire to know my paternal roots led to research in which I found Joseph Byard, my great-great grandfather in Early County, Blakely, GA. According to the 1870 United States Census, Early County was another hot bed for the KKK during those times. The 1870 Census was the first time when blacks were listed by name, instead of property. However, Joseph's birthplace was indicated as the West Indies, in 1810. Further research of the 1860 Census revealed that his age corresponded with a pair of slaves, out of several hundred, who were owned by a Doctor Hill on or near the same property. I have no idea why Byard, and not Hill, became my family's surname immediately after slavery.

Joseph's union with Hannah, for whom I was unable to locate information, other than her age, produced several daughters and one son, William, my great grandfather.

William, also born a slave, united with Catherine, for whom I also have no knowledge other than her age, produced several daughters and two sons, including my grandfather, Admus.

10

I Love America But America Don't Love Me

Admus united with my paternal grandma, Sadie Armstrong. Sadie was the daughter of Eugene Armstrong, the son of freed slaves, Sam and Dolly, my great-great-grandfather and great-great-grandmother and Docia Densler who was the daughter of freed slaves, James Denslow and Louisa Densler. Admus and Sadie's union produced one daughter and six sons, including my father, Eddie "C," the oldest of 7. I believe that all but the youngest, my uncle James, was born in Early County, GA. I'm not sure what year or what the circumstances were for Admus to change our surname from Byard to Byirt. However, one suggestion was that since he never learned to read or write, perhaps a Census-taker wrote his name like she felt she heard it. Another suggestion was that my Uncle Arthur's untimely death and the events after, precipitated the change and the move to Dawson as the Byirts.

However, the Byirts stayed in Dawson long enough before moving on to Delray Beach, Florida in their quest to get to the West Indies for my father, Eddie "C." Byirt Sr.to unite with my momma, Annie Will Crumbley and 2 other ladies. From these unions, there were two daughters and three sons produced. My sister Brenda and I are his children by Ann. He has a set of twins with Ms. Dorothy

I Love America But America Don't Love Me

Hunt, my sister Martha and my brother Marvin. I also have a brother named Eddie B; whose mother is Ms. Susie Watson. Each year on my birthday, the four of us are all the same age. However, I didn't get a chance to meet my siblings until I was around 20 years old. But blood is thick, and the Love is there.

When I was born my Grandpa Admus was the Byirt in charge. I would never get to witness my grandfather Admus in action, but I did witness some results. I was told that he was a spirited and fiery man, he had a sharp eye, kept a sharp lookout and a razor-sharp knife. I heard once there was a rift between the Crumbleys and Byirts in which my grandfather stabbed and cut one of my cousins from the other side within an inch of his life. My grandfather didn't discriminate though. My grandmother, his wife, my father and Uncle J D experienced his wrath. They all survived, forgave and let live. After spending months in the hospital, my grandmother faithfully came back home.

As I mentioned before, my grandfather kept a sharp lookout. I'm told that the first time he ever saw the ocean, in a panic, he took off running while warning other family members present to run too because, "that thing is about to spill over," when he saw a big wave on the horizon.

On another occasion while Delray Beach Police were attempting to arrest him, he warned them that they had no jurisdiction over him because he worked for the City government, just like they did. He was a Sanitation Engineer (Garbage Man).

He was truly a spirited and feisty man who when he died at the age of 86, was blind and rolling two bullets in his hand, and had his razor-sharp blade at his side. Some of the things I heard that my granddaddy and uncles did for our family to survive in the 'Jungle of Racism,' would make a lot of men cringe. I'm glad that gene had somewhat dissipated by the time I was born.

Please walk with me through the pages of this book, inspired by the blood within me, from my great-great grandfather, Joseph Byard, who was born in the West Indies, the true and authentic Native Americans, and all the others who united to produce me. All of them is me!! This is who I am, and America has not always been kind. However, I don't have a hateful a hateful bone in my body or any will that is ill. Instead, I am a man of principles with a solid moral compass and Love in my Heart. By no means am I holier than thou, merely a product of my environment and circumstances.

I Love America But America Don't Love Me

Picture America as the factory and me the product going through (enduring) systematic racism, high-tech lynching's, and other challenges as I've pursued Life, Liberty and Happiness. Unlike Jadakiss and Anthony Hamilton in their song, I never thought to ask the question "Why." Eventually, I just internalized everything happening to me and around me and decided to just keep my guard up.

CHAPTER 1

My mom Annie, having fled the Byirts and their (rowdy ways) including my father Eddie C., Sr. in Delray Beach, Florida, and the atrocities bestowed on black people in search of a better way of life, was hustling me and my little sister Brenda along the streets of Rockford, IL one bright, sunny day.

It was our first time downtown there and the buildings seemed so much taller than the ones I remembered in Delray Beach and Dawson. I'd never seen so many white people at one time in my life. As we walked along the sidewalk, out of nowhere, a little white girl who appeared to be about my age blurted out, "Mommy,

mommy, look at the Niggers." Instantly, my mom asserted, "Your mommy is the nigger," as the little girls' mom embarrassingly tried to hush her and move past us.

My mother, thinking we were escaping racism by leaving the South, was shaken up enough for me to realize and also heartbroken to encounter another form of the same obstacle that she had tried to leave behind and protect me and my sister from. I guess I'd been pretty much protected from racism, but I got my first brush with it in 1960 when I was five years old. The little girl was just as innocent as me, but the seeds of racism had been planted and sowed already in our short lives. The little girl had obviously only repeated what she'd heard, giving credence to the statement, "Racism is a learned behavior, people are not born racist."

We settled in at our Uncle Albert (my mom's fathers' brother) and Aunt Frances' home. They had moved north a few years earlier, mainly for Aunt Frances to be closer to their only child, Essie, from whom They'd been separated from shortly after birth. But they also welcomed the opportunities they hoped they would find.

Their house was on Newport Road in the West End. It was a

small three-bedroom bungalow but clean and very well kept. The neighborhood was probably 75% black folks.

My mom found work like many other young black women who moved from the south seeking work opportunities in the north, at a poultry farm on Rockford's outskirts, You would immediately know that they worked there if you ran into them on the streets. The smell that they carried with them when they left the farm was powerful and undeniable. Really, Rockford was just a big southern country town located in the north.

I attended kindergarten at Concord Community Center and from there I went to William Dennis Elementary School. I was only in the second or third grade, but my most vivid memory there was the assassination of the Honorable John Fitzgerald Kennedy. Everyone mourned the President's death. I can remember hearing some of the adults suggesting, and some swearing, that the President was assassinated because he was too friendly to blacks, sympathetic to their causes, and doing too much to help them. Generally, they all seemed to hurt and wondered out loud sometimes, "Lord what is the world coming to?"

I Love America But America Don't Love Me

During the next summer, my sister, mom and my mom's best friend, Gloria Johnson, joined Aunt Frances and Uncle Albert for their vacation. We all hopped in the old Ford and headed south. I remember seeing a "Whites Only" sign at a gas station that we stopped at along the way and a very prominent sign with an arrow that read, "Negroes" that pointed to the back of the building. I guess I wasn't quite old enough to comprehend the true meaning of the signs because when I got inside the gas station, I drank me some of that white water. Nobody said nothing to me. But before we could get out of the parking lot, according to the adults present, the store employees appeared to be dismantling the fountain from which I drank. Later, my Mom said she had never seen Gloria laugh so hard.

After staying with Uncle Albert and Aunt Frances for a good while, my Mom finally earned enough money to rent a room in a big house that was turned into a "rooming house" on Blinn Court on Rockford's northwest side. This neighborhood's demographics was probably 50% black and 50% white.

It was only a room, but it was our first place where my mom was responsible for paying the rent. There was a shared kitchen and bathroom, but it was neat and clean. My mom still managed to get me to school at William Dennis as well for a while. My little sister and I liked the location just fine. We got to eat those delicious hamburgers and awesome French fries from a place called Geri's that was not too far away from where we lived. But the best thing from Geri's, in my opinion, was the strawberry milkshakes.

Our time on Blinn Court turned out to be no more than a pit stop. After only a couple of months, my mom found a better job, so we were able to move into a two-bedroom apartment on Rockford's southside on Ferguson Street, across from Saint Anthony's Catholic Church and School. The neighborhood there was mostly a mix of black, Italian, white and a couple of Mexican families. The building had five apartments and all the occupants were black except for one, that was occupied by a mixed-race Goddess. Everybody that lived there was like one big happy family. A teenaged boy named Day-Day Johnson lived in one of the apartments with his mother, Ms. Lil. I was too young to know what was really going on, but it seemed like Day-Day and his friends were always fighting against the Italian and white boys in the neighborhood. One night, Day-Day was seriously injured by a stab wound in his side, but it didn't keep him down long. Before anybody knew it, he was up and running around the block on his hands again. Truly a character.

The thing that made this location so extra cool for me was the Dariette down on the corner. You could get a hamburger, French fries and a Coke for 37 cents, and an assortment of flavored Granitas for a dime.

The designated school was O.F. Barbour. Because of my limited knowledge at the time regarding sex and having babies, one day in school, I called my teacher, a young pregnant white woman, "nasty." She slapped the taste out of my mouth, so I slapped her back, just as the Principal opened the classroom door. My mom had told me that if anybody other than her put their hands on me, to hit 'em back, so I did. I was removed from her class and I never saw her again.

My best friends at the time were Hiram David and Oscar Tripplett. Oscar lived three blocks up the street where the street name changed from Ferguson to Donaldsen. Oscar always stopped by in the morning and we would start out walking to school together and be joined by other friends along the way. My friends were both black Mexican and white. In those days, children spent most daylight hours outside playing. But there came a time when I noticed that whenever my white friends came to my house, they could come in if they wanted to. But whenever I went to one of their houses, I always had to wait outside. I, nor my white friends, I don't think knew it at that time, but racism was being taught and practiced.

Booker T. Washington's (BWC) Community Recreation Center was about three blocks to the east on Kent Street. Oscar, the Lee brothers, Shane and Mike, Gerald Floyd and I spent a lot of time there whenever I could go. Even though the neighborhood was mixed, I don't remember any white kids ever attending the Center.

In 1966 when I was 11 years old, word got around that Booker Washington was starting their first ever little league baseball team. I tried out and made the team. All our players were black and most of us had never played in a real game. Most of us were softball pros, but this was fast pitch, hard ball.

Mr. Zachary was our coach and his eldest son John, served as his assistant coach. His youngest son Lynn played on the team. The star on our team was Overtis Patterson, a pitcher/outfielder who had previously played in real games. Also, on the team were the Meeks brothers, Junior and Tommy, Alfred Marshall, Greg Zachery, Mike

Sallis, Larry Bowden, I think the Lee Brothers, Shane and Mike and my first Cousin Luther Crumbley, III. For those whose names elude me, forgive me, this is a few years later.

After a few practices and everybody had won or earned their position, our first game came around. Mr. Zachary and John was most of our transportation to and from the games.

When we got there, we saw that BWC was the only all black team, but there were some teams that had one, two or three black players at the max. I saw one of my close friends from school, Hiram David, with his father Luke who was said to have Major League Baseball skills, but somehow never got the opportunity to play at that level. Himey was his team's only black player. He played the shortstop position and had flair for the position. A couple of years later whenever he took the field, someone would always yell out, "Himey, you got your make up on?" Watching him play was a thing of beauty.

There were five or six baseball diamonds at the field and games were being played on all of them. When it was time for our game, a little crowd gathered. I started at second base. At one point in the game, a Latham Tool player hit the ball over the outfield fence on the fly. I started yelling in panic mode at my outfielder who was closest to where the ball went out, to go get the ball. Him, knowing it was a home run, just stood there. But I took off running, in panic mode, toward right center field, leapt the fence in one motion, retrieved the ball and threw it back toward the infield only a second or two after the hitter crossed the plate. Only then did I realize that all the white people were laughing, but I didn't know why. Mr. Zachary, who didn't see the humor in my actions, called timeout to explain to me the rules regarding balls that were hit over the fence. It was my first game and I didn't know. Recently, I asked Luther if he remembered that day. He said, "yes cuz, I thought you was within your rights too," and we both laughed. I was trying to get him.

Anyway, late in the game when we were down to our last at-bat, Larry was determined to score. I got a hit with him on first base. My hit flew to left center field and we thought we had a chance to score. Their outfielder got the ball and threw it to the third baseman with Larry coming towards him a mere second after the ball got there. As he neared the third baseman who was waiting with the ball, he decided to kick his way into the base and hopefully past third. But that was our last out in an ass whooping that seemed to be to the delight of everyone white. They laughed and ridiculed some little black boys who had never played in an organized league game. When the Mercy Rule came into effect, the final score was Latham Tool -21-Booker Washington Center-0. I have never forgotten it!

As the season went on, me and my teammates got better at baseball and came to understand some of the rules of the game. We won some games, and as a result of our improvement, we became familiar with sayings like, "Y'all playing against the umpires too" or, "it's eleven against nine." As I became more and more aware of the discrepancy, I wondered why? I didn't have a crooked bone in my body or soul. We hadn't done anybody any wrong. However, most calls always seemed to favor the white teams.

The team concept and competition of basketball and baseball held my interest. So, I began to devote more time to these two sports, and at the center. This dedication separated me even more from my white friends in the neighborhood.

Right before I was to begin junior high school at George Washington whose mascot was the Minutemen, we moved to 1515 Clifton Road, a three-bedroom upstairs apartment, still on the south side of town. Mrs. Ruth Hudson and her five daughters stayed

I Love America But America Don't Love Me

downstairs. Future West High Basketball great, Center, Greg Wells' family lived next door. The Simmons, the Ausler, and Jefferson families lived across the street.

When I got to Washington Jr. High, I remained friends with my white friends. But they started hanging out more with new white friends and I fell right in line with the old saying, "Birds of a feather flock together." I met new friends Arthur Fulson, Phillip Hubbard, Will Mac Roby, Gus Waller and others.

My mom started preaching to me early on about responsibility and strong work ethics, so I had various odd jobs, like newspaper boy, I cut grass in my neighborhood as well as shoveling snow. I was also known as a 'Pop Bottle Hustler' and I collected them anywhere I could find them, including the alleys in the neighborhood where other opportunities and values were often found. Later, I worked a job called 'Street Treat Boy.' I rode a bicycle with a refrigerator attached on wheels, selling ice cream and popsicles. I gave away as many popsicles as I sold, but never once came up short on the money.

I still found the time to play basketball at school and in the recreation league. However. baseball was my game and like most of

I Love America But America Don't Love Me

our players, I continued to play for BWC after the team changed leagues.

In the spring of 1968, the Reverend Dr. Martin Luther King Jr. was murdered. Before Dr. King was killed, Washington Jr. High's racial mix was probably as high as 70/30-white to black. The next day of school after his murder, several fights broke out at school and I witnessed chaos amongst the students. I couldn't feel any anger at anybody near me because no one I knew had killed Dr. King or offended me.

For the following two weeks, most of the black students went to Pilgrim's Baptist Church for school. Only then did we learn about the 16th Street Baptist Church bombing in 1963 in Birmingham, the lynching of 14-year old Emmitt Till in 1955 in Mississippi, the murders of Chaney, Goodman and Schwerner, three activists, during the Freedom Summer of 1964 in Mississippi, Bloody Sunday in Alabama, and the reason for the riots in Watts, California and Detroit. When we returned to Washington Jr. High, many of the white students did not.

Later in the year, Dr. King's confidant, Reverend Ralph David Abernathy came to our school with a new program called,

I Love America But America Don't Love Me

"Operation Breadbasket." Operation Breadbasket was organized and dedicated to improving the economic conditions of black communities across the United States of America.

On this day, all of the students were ushered in to the school auditorium where I listened quietly and fully focused on Reverend Abernathy's message, "I may be poor, but I am somebody; I may be black, but I am somebody; I may not drive a new fancy car, but I am somebody. Even though I never felt less than anyone, I put on a coat of armor. I had concluded that even though I Loved America, America Didn't Love Me. However, I left school that day black and proud as I had ever been.

In June, Robert F Kennedy, President J.F. Kennedy's brother, also a pro black politician, was assassinated and most black Americans mourned again for a fallen hero.

In the summer of 1968, James Brown recorded the song, "Say it Loud, I'm Black and I'm Proud." The song became the black man's anthem for the times. After Say it Loud, a few artist, Sonny Charles (Black Pearl), Jerry Butler (Only the Strong Survive), and others recorded songs dedicated to the struggle for equality throughout America. Many of the songs inspired, gave black people hope, soothed and played a major part in black folk's ability to cope.

Until just recently did I gain knowledge about the protest that happened outside of West High School on April 25, 1969, the spring before I was to begin there in the fall when 40 of about 200 black people were arrested while peacefully protesting that the school had no black cheerleaders, no black counselors or teachers, and because they wanted black history to be taught by black teachers, and equal rights pertaining to school activity. Their bond was set at $25.00, but Grayned, who I believe had a couple of sisters attending West, decided to fight the power and the case made its way to the Supreme Court. The case, Grayned v. Rockford, IL, was settled in 1972.

Right before my freshman year at Rockford West High School, I found out that the school boundaries had been changed and some of my closest friends like Will Mac Roby, Shane and Mike Lee, the Woolfork and Patterson brothers, amongst others, would not be transitioning with us to the same school. We were divided. If we had all been allowed to attend together, West might have dominated at least two of the three major sports for four years. In one sense, we were divided and conquered at that point.

Chapter 2

When school started, it was football season and some of the guys that I had played with and against in sandlot games, and even a time or two on concrete, talked me into trying out for the team. I did and I made it. At the time, I didn't have a special love for the game outside of watching the ferocity in which the Chicago Bears' great middle linebacker, Dick Butkus played with. I welcomed the companionship of my friends on the team and the high-spirited competition of the game.

In preparation for the season, we played a practice game against a catholic school, I believe it was Lutheran. All their players were white. In the game, I was handed the ball five times at different yard lines on the field, and all five times I scored. After the game, I overheard the other team's coach ask my Coach Anderson what kind of name is Byirt, where did he come from and tell him, "that boy is really going to hurt somebody."

After a conference between West Football Coaches', though I'd never played football for a team, I was labeled as "not being smart enough to remember plays," therefore I couldn't play running back. What I wasn't smart enough to see was the racism behind their decision and their fear about the mystery in Byirt.

I still was able to earn a starting spot on the defensive line, which was fine by me. I just wanted to be on the team. The glory positions being reserved for my white teammates never crossed my mind.

When basketball season rolled around, all the core guys except Gus, but including me who had played for Washington Jr. High, made the team.

It was during this season that Marcus Clark and Fred Hampton, two leaders of the Black Panther Party, whose mission was economic equality, equal opportunity and racial justice, were

I Love America But America Don't Love Me

murdered 90 miles away in Chicago, Illinois in their sleep on December 4th, 1969, The Chicago Police, FBI and ATF Forces stormed their homes in the wee hours of the morning. Nothing changed in Rockford, and life went on as usual.

I made the freshman baseball team when the season rolled around but played sparingly. Even though I had always started in the summer leagues, it was hard for me to get on the diamond at West.

The next summer league baseball for me was in the Colt League. In order to play in the league, players had to go to a big try-out to display their skills and ultimately be drafted by a team that liked what they saw in a player. I was drafted by a team named the West End Businessman. The owner was a nice Chinese man named Mr. Jack Oshita. He owned a dry cleaner on West State Street. He also had a daughter, Amy, who was a classmate at West High.

The coach was a white attorney. His first name was Mr., and last name was Cook. He was a good man though. He had a son whose name I don't remember, that played legion ball. He was pretty good, and he did some coaching too.

Upon my arrival at the first practice with the West End

I Love America But America Don't Love Me

Businessman, it didn't look like the West End I knew, and it didn't have the West End feel. I saw that there was only one other black player, Michael Harris, I believe his name was, and he was the product of a bi-racial relationship.

By opening day, I'd won a starting position and in my first game on my very first trip to the bench from the field, a white teammate from Loves Park quickly moved over from the spot he was sitting to the spot I started to sit in saying, "Go to the end of the bench where Niggers belong." Without so much as a thought, but with lightning fast precision and power, I hit him square in his face, breaking his nose and shattering facial bones.

I was already feeling uncomfortable because me and Harris were the only two black people in the park that day. Hearing those words from my teammate shined a light on the situation and it was more than I could bear.

He was rushed to the hospital with serious injuries, and if not for his timely arrival at the hospital, he could have died that day. After everybody told their version of the story about how and what happened, I wasn't punished. But when my mom heard about it, she got all nervous and scared. She made me visit him in the hospital

32

and take him candy and flowers. Years later when I asked my mom why she made me do that, she said that she genuinely felt sorry for him but that she was also afraid of having to pay his doctor bills for the rest of her life.

My teammate didn't get off the disabled list that year and didn't return for the second year of Colt ball. After the incident, the rest of my teammates all embraced me and nothing else was ever said about it.

This was the summer of 1970 when on August 7th, there was an attempted prison break in Sole Dad, California, in which the death of four people, including a Judge, occurred as a result of three black inmates who were murdered by the guards, for protesting existing and racial conflicts.

The following football season, my sophomore year, was different. Even though I was relegated to the defensive tackle position, and not quite 6 feet tall yet and 170 pounds, I was the team's defensive leader and leading tackler. I was fine with it. I had no problems with my teammates scoring the touchdowns and receiving the glory because I was able to crack heads and inflict pain, legally. It didn't matter, black or white. It was all in the game.

I Love America But America Don't Love Me

In one game, on three consecutive plays, the opposing team's quarterback, halfback, and fullback all suffered injuries, and had to be removed from the game as a result of tackles made by me. Dick Butkus was my idol and I played like him.

Football was not at first perceived as but proved to be a great outlet to vent my frustrations as I tried to comprehend and deal with the injustices that had occurred in my life and around me. Our team did well but I always felt that we would have been better if they had let me carry the ball.

After football season was over, it was time to switch balls. But as soon as I stepped through the doors to the basketball court, Richard Staas' the head sophomore coach, approached me and told me that I couldn't even try-out for his team. The reason that he used was the 'bad attitude' wrench, and at 15 years of age, any chance I had at a basketball career quickly disappeared and I became unworthy and too old for an 'attitude adjustment if that was the case. He took the ball out my hand at age 15 and handed it to his son at a level he didn't deserve to play other than being the coach's son. What if it had been a black coach who told a 15-year-old white boy that he couldn't even set foot on the court and try out for his team.

Better yet, what if that had been a black coach telling his own boy that. Standing at only about 5' 10", I'd recently dunked for the first time following a brick free throw and Gus and myself were one of two guys on the team that could go toe-to-toe with Ernie Kent, a West High Star who eventually went on to the University of Oregon on a basketball scholarship.

I was hurt, but I didn't allow him the pleasure of seeing my pain and disappointment. My path was altered because over the past three years, I'd formed friendships and relationships with my teammates and had always been one of my team's first six players in recreation and school ball. But this season, Coach Staas' son was an incoming freshman who needed a spot on the team. So, he was elevated and my spot on the team became his son's spot.

My mom was all about work, wasn't interested in sports, and I didn't have a hands-on dad or anyone else to help me sort out the things coming at me in a racist society, or to help me rectify this injustice. I venture to say I could go get four more guys, a couple going to West and a couple out the rec league and beat the brakes off the school team even though they had Himey and Ernie and fared well in school competition. Color still played a huge part at West when I went through.

I turned 16 when February came, and through a friend of the family from church, Deacon Robert Jones, my friend Dallas' Dad, I got a job at a Metal Heat Treating Plant in Loves Park as a day watchman. My hours were from 6AM to 6PM on Saturday and Sunday. That tour of duty ended on a Saturday morning when one of the owners came in and caught me sound asleep in the locker room. "Wake the fuck up, Nigger." I woke up, said nothing and headed for the telephone as Mr. Charlie followed behind me, still spewing racial slurs. My mom had basically set the job up, so I called her, "Momma, Mr. Charlie called me a Nigger." Instead of her telling me to try and whoop his ass, she said, "You tell him to kiss your black ass, I'll be there in a minute," and she was on her way. Before he could say another word, "Kiss my black ass, your fat ass honkey," I told him as I hung the phone up to leave. My mom was there from across town, seemingly before I could get the words out of my mouth.

I was remorseful though about losing my job because the pay was good for a 16-year-old. Even though no harm was done, the fact remained that I had been asleep on the job. My mom reasoned that going to school all week and working 24 of the 48 hours on the weekend might be a bit much for baby boy to bear.

Baseball season came. The freshman/sophomore team was average, but the varsity team won the sectional title in a game played in Elgin, Illinois, about 45 miles and an hours' drive from Rockford.

In my excitement after the game, I forgot to use the restroom before boarding the bus for our return trip to Rockford, and there were no restrooms on school buses. We were only about 10 to 15 minutes into the ride, everybody was happy, excited and celebrating the victory when I had to pee.

When I felt like I couldn't hold it any longer, I yelled to the front of the bus, "Coach, coach, I got to pee!" "Tie it in a knot, I've seen it and it's long enough," Coach Schwalbach, answered for Coach Charlie Wild, and the bus erupted with laughter and joy again. I painfully suffered as we rode on.

A few minutes later, I felt like I would surely burst and maybe pee on myself. "Coach, coach please, I got to use the bathroom really bad." Coach Wild responded this time, "Do it in your clothes, I'll take the blame." Laughter broke out again and we rode on.

I Love America But America Don't Love Me

The bus was working its way along East State Street, one of the busiest streets in town, when I just couldn't hold my pee anymore. I sprang to my feet, made it to an open window, hung my inches out and started pissing, oblivious to the world.

The bus got quiet. Schwalbach and Wild looked back, "He isn't?" Coach Wild asked. "He is," Coach Schwalbach answered. Coach Wild then asked, "What kind of animal are you?" "A black animal," I shot back. For that offense, I was suspended from all school sports for my entire junior year. Looking back, the right thing for me to have done was piss on the floor. But in hindsight, I was too scared to mess up them white folk's school bus.

By the second year of Colt baseball with West End Businessmen, I was considered a good hitter and had never struck out more than five times in a season. But the lefty that we faced in this game had previously struck me out three times, including once in this game. In this at-bat, I was one strike away from strike out number four. His curve ball was awesome. The pitch would come in eye-high and outside, then dive right across the heart of the plate. The next pitch started to come in the same way, but I jumped the pitch before it's break, then crack, boom, bop pow! Everybody in the stands stood up, 'oohing and 'ahhhing, and in the stands behind me, I heard a white man say, "I know the Nigger wishes he could've straightened that one out." I hit the ball an estimated 500 ft, an incredible feat for any man, let alone a 16-year-old boy. But I hit it foul. On the very next pitch coming in the same way I swung and missed. "STRIIIIKE THREE," the umpire yelled. Damn, he got me again, I thought to myself. Just like life in a racist society, the curve balls keep coming in at eye-level and sweeping low.

Chapter 3

When school started back, I was separated from my student/athlete friends once again, due to a year-long suspension. I started hanging out with my other friends and the three of us, Art F and Hilton, got jobs at O'Donalds' a local grocery store on South Main. The money wasn't as good as at the plant, but all was going well until one of our white friends started working there for more pay and an easier job. He liked to rub our faces in it. He never did use the magic word, but one day we locked up in the storage room. He held his own and we later became good friends.

While I was suspended from sports, I got serious enough

about girls to impregnate my high school sweetie. She had just turned 16 and I'd just turned 17. With a baby on the way and responsibilities looming, I needed a better job and Deacon Jones arranged for me to be rehired at the same plant where Mr. Charlie, one of the owners, had called me a Nigger, and who I told to kiss my black ass. During my entire employment both times, I may have seen him all of three times.

This tour of duty was different, however. I went to school full time and worked full time as a machine operator from 3PM to 11PM Monday - Friday, making grown man money and more than my mom.

I managed to stay out of trouble and when the year-long suspension from sports had past, I was eligible to play football again when school started. However, during summer session football practice, trouble found me again. In between sessions one day, I don't remember whose idea it was, but me, Mike, Art C, the two starting halfbacks, and Dave, who should have been the starting QB, got caught stealing five cases of beer out of a warehouse across the street from where the Rockford Peaches Women's Professional Baseball team had played from 1943-1954. It was called Beyer

Stadium then.

Mike, Art C, and I, the three black boys went to jail, but Dave got a ride home. When we saw him again, he told us that during the ride home that the police warned him about hanging with his black friends and joked about us going to jail and him getting a ride home.

It was my first time going to jail, but when my mom found her way to me, at first sight, she fired on me saying she could understand if I got caught stealing if I was hungry, but since it was beer, I could stay down there in jail, and she left. I thank God for my Aunt Lil because had it not been for her, I might still be in jail.

When news got back to the coaches, it was decided that everybody, except me, could play that season, my senior year and my last season. I was heartbroken. Within a week's time, one of my white teammates, Al Benz's father, went to bat for me and I was allowed back on the team. Today, I'm still grateful.

My next adventure came one day when me, Mike and Art C was at one of our white female classmate's home with two of her white girlfriends, enjoying the indoor swimming pool while her parents were away. Unexpectedly, her mom came home and walked

42

in to find three young white girls and three young black boys running around in bikinis and swimming trunks. She didn't say a word as we all started scrambling to get dried and dressed. She just sat down at a table and started crying as if someone dear to her had just passed away. She cried so hard and with so much pain, it affected me and almost made me cry. I never saw my friend at school or anywhere else, ever again.

After missing my junior year of football, I was still my team's defensive leader and I led the team, and maybe the league, in tackles from the nose guard position. But I knew in my heart that our team would be even better if I had been allowed to run the ball and play the middle linebacker position. The positions that were being played by Al, the son of the man who made it possible for me to play that year and backed up by a true friend that was white and died way too young, Spencer Anderson.

Early in the season, Mike Sallis, who was also on Booker Washington's first baseball team ever, was a starting halfback, went down in a game. Then Al went down and a game later, Spencer, Al's backup, went down too and so did expectations for our season. But with me leading the defense, we came within one game of having a three-way tie for first place.

We lost our homecoming game by one point, 7-6, on the last play of the game. In the game, I forced a couple of fumbles and was credited with only 17 tackles playing the nose guard position and weighing 175 pounds and standing 6 feet tall. Because of my strength and my quickness, most of the time I was in the backfield at the same time the ball was being handed off, wreaking havoc and making tackles.

However, on the last play of the game, their center and both guards' assignment was to triple team me, grab and hold me at any cost. At the snap of the ball, the three of them converged, holding me as the ball carrier swept to my left off the right hash mark, all while the referee watched them holding me. Everybody in the stadium saw this happening, but the ref didn't make the call. Their ball carrier was met by our cornerback, Double H, at about the two-yard line, but he plowed over anyway for a game tying touchdown, resulting in a game ending and winning the extra point.

West ruled for 47 minutes and 59 seconds, only to have the game snatched by a dirty and illegal play. That troubled me deeply. I knew we didn't get that last call, as evident as it was, because the

44

other team and the referees were all white. It affected me bad and I moped about during the following days. I knew that loss was the best game that I had ever played. But most of all, I hurt because I didn't come through for my school, my teammates and friends in our homecoming game.

That Wednesday, while in the school library reading the Rockford Register Star, like I'd grown accustomed to, I was shocked but pleasantly surprised when I saw my picture and a large newspaper article on the front page of the Sports Section that read, "Byirt Picks up Slack for Warriors." I thought to myself, damn, I wasn't the only one who recognized that I had played my heart out. The newspaper article, however, was just a consolation prize for not getting that hold call and missing out on a win that would have ultimately led to a three-way tie for first place in the Big Nine. I cut the article out and I still have it. A copy of it follows:

Photo provided courtesy of Rockford Register Star and rrstar.com

At football seasons' end, I realized that we could have won all our games if not for racism, inside and outside of school. During my time in high school, we missed out on a few championships in all the sports because of the extreme current of racism. I learned that White Supremacy at most times outweighed morals, ethics, championships, and even winning.

When the season was over, I resumed my schedule at the Metal Heat Treating Plant and continued to go to school. On

I Love America But America Don't Love Me

December 5th, I became a high school Dad. My high school sweetie blessed me with a baby boy.

As for football, I was slightly marketed and therefore lightly recruited, but I did visit some small schools in Illinois and Wisconsin. By the end of school, I had decided on a small school, Milton in Wisconsin. Coming from where I'm from, even then, I never dreamed of playing professional football. But Milton has produced one a pretty good QB, David Krieg.

I was all set to go when I learned that two of my white teammates, including one who was behind me on the depth chart, were receiving full scholarships to Milton, but I was only offered half a ride. I thought about my mom not being able to pay for me to go to school and take care of my baby. I felt like it was another shot of racism and that it just wasn't right. So, I decided not to go to college and accept this unfair discrepancy. If there was one thing in life that I could do over, I would start here.

College started for my friends while I languished at the heat-treating plant. And I went to work faithfully. But around late August, early September, I began to develop a real ugly rash on both of my thighs, due to oil splashing on me through my pants while I worked around certain machines.

I was still hurting and feeling dejected and sorry for myself when I got the word that the recruiter from the Marine Corps had been around to my mom's house a couple of times, looking for me. I decided to go visit the Recruiting Office, taking Oscar, our Mexican friend, Frank and Art F with me. Oscar and Frank had both lost older brothers to the War in Vietnam.

The four of us went to visit the recruiters three or four times. When it was time for us to decide, Oscar decided he wasn't going. And because Frank was only 17, he needed his parent's signature to enlist, but they wouldn't give him their permission. Art needed his parent's signature too, but they signed the form quickly. Art and I signed up and we were joined by Barry Fletcher, a friend from school who lived on the north side to a three-part Buddy Program. The only thing it means is that you go through boot camp together. So, it was on September 27, 1973, that we decided to go serve our country via the United States Marine Corps.

CHAPTER 4

As Art and I walked through the corridors of O'Hare Airport in Chicago on the way to our first flight ever, a real tall man was attracting a lot of attention, but no was approaching him. When we got closer, we saw that it was Kareem Abdul Jabbar. Foolishly and excitedly, I approached him asking, "are you Lew Alcindor?" "No," he answered. I asked him again. "No, I'm not Lew Alcindor," he answered again. Dumbfounded, I thought that there was no way there could be two folks in the world who looked so much alike. He went into a small eatery along the corridor, so I followed him in. "Man, you know you Lew Alcindor." His reply this time was not so nice, and I got the message, which was get out my face and leave me

49

alone. Of course, I complied. But on the way out of the eatery, and barely loud enough for him to hear, I said, "I know you Lew Alcindor."

Growing up in Rockford where black news always got to us late, if at all, I was green and uninformed. I didn't realize until later that it was Kareem's rejection of a slave name and mentality, and that he in fact had changed his name. I still had a bad taste in my mouth for a long time, one that didn't get sweeter until Magic Johnson teamed up and seemed to soften him a bit with the Laker's and Showtime. I had to root for them. If I could talk to Kareem right now, I'd apologize and tell him, 'man, I didn't know what you had been going through and that I meant no disrespect.'

Our flight was at night. We couldn't see anything out the window, so the flight from Chicago, Illinois to San Diego, California was otherwise uneventful.

At the airport in San Diego, we met a lot more recruits, some of them were on their way to Navy Boot Camp. All the Marine Corps recruits were gathered, and then led to our respective buses for transfer to Marine Corps Recruit Division (MCRD). After me, Art and Barry got to our bus and the doors were shut, the five or six regular Marines already aboard started yelling at us, "shut the f up, shut the f up, don't say another word." And everybody obeyed. We rode along in silence, and no one said peep. I was thinking to myself, "what have I got us into?" and that the Marines at the recruiting office was so much nicer than these Marines.

When the bus pulled up outside the barbershop on the base and stopped, several Marines wearing smokie's rushed the buses yelling, "Get off the f-ing bus and into those footprints over by the barbershop door." We were all confused and shocked but, every recruit ran for their lives and filled up the footprints.

One by one, we were all led inside where all of us were shaved bald. When Art got in the barber's chair, he began to tell him how to cut his hair. He told him to leave three inches on top and to trim (evenly graduated) down the sides. The barber listened, said okay, and made his first pass right down the middle of Art's afro. The afro he was so black and proud of. If looks could kill, I would have died that day on the spot, judging from the glare on his face when he looked at me. The recruiter had assured him that an official Marine Corps haircut allowed only three inches on top, and evenly graduated on the sides. The catch was that we weren't Marines yet.

I Love America But America Don't Love Me

As each new recruit's hair was cut, we were led into an adjacent room where we shed our civilian clothes all the way down to our underwear and put them in boxes with mothballs. Then we were issued new underwear, very wrinkled fatigue green uniforms, cap included, wool green socks and black combat boots.

After each recruit got his head shaved and dressed out, under a stern command for silence, filled up the footprints again and waited until the regular drill instructors came to get the recruits who would form the next Marine Corps recruit training battalion. However, there was a problem with Art, Barry, and me regarding the Buddy Program. According to our recruiter, there were only two slots left to complete 3rd battalion to begin training as scheduled and be home for Christmas. Because Barry had been added to our Buddy Plan, we would have to spend an extra 18 days in forming, waiting for the 1st Battalion to form.

On our first day in forming, I approached a drill instructor and asked, "Hey man, where is the bathroom?" With cobra-like quickness, he grabbed me by the throat and asked, "What did you just call me? You ask if you can talk to me. There is no such thing as a bathroom, it's called the head." Moving his grip from my throat, he continued, "The first word and the last word out of your mouth will be Sir." I didn't know exactly how far this place was from Rockford, but I knew it took a plane to get me there, and if I wanted to get back, maybe I better sit back.

Seeing what happened to me put all the other recruits on alert. Later that evening, I saw another recruit who had to use the head. Looking like a deer caught in headlights, he crouched low and crept to a spot out of the drill instructor's sight, wrapped his penis in a big towel and let himself go. I guess he be damned if he was going to have a run-in like mine.

The entire 18 days consisted of policing the area and picking up trash, including cigarette butts. Most days, we were in bed by 5 PM and told not to socialize or talk to anybody.

I managed not to get attacked again. But on the day that Sergeant Watson came to pick up the recruits for his platoon, including the trio from Rockford, on the way out the drill instructor who'd grabbed me by the throat, told Sergeant Watson, "You got a smart ass private there." Sergeant Watson told him something like, "you don't mess with my recruits." And since I saw that, I thought I had back-up. I never said a word, but I believe that the drill instructor knew from the look I put on my face and my demeanor, that if we were any place else, he'd have his hands full.

Upon arrival to our barracks where we would live and train for the next 80 days, we met all four of our drill instructors. All four of them claimed that for the next 80 days, they would be our mothers and our fathers and the other recruits our sisters and brothers. Training began with over 70 recruits. Art was chosen to be one of the four squad leaders. Me and a big Samoan guy, whose name I believe was Leiuta, were assigned the title of 'Warlords'. We were told that our job would be anything that the squad leaders and guide couldn't handle as far as keeping the recruits in line when no drill instructor was present. Neither of us ever had to act in that capacity, as far as I know.

Staff Sergeant Bryant, who was black, was Platoon1101's lead drill instructor. He was a man who I looked up to and held in high esteem. He earned a Silver Star Medal for his heroics in the War in Vietnam. And the way he wore his uniform, I believe was like a picture-perfect poster Marine. Some days though, Staff Sergeant Bryant looked troubled, and on some occasions when we would be training and an airplane flew over, he would drop to the ground and start firing at the plane with his imaginary weapon. I didn't know back then, but I know now that behavior is called Post Traumatic Stress Syndrome.

Staff Sergeant Marsh, who was also black, was also a Vietnam War Veteran. He looked and played the part of a squared away Marine Corps drill instructor. Most of the time while we were training, SSgt. Marsh sparred performing karate on an imaginary opponent. Whenever the opportunity presented itself, and there were plenty of those moments, he would stand sideways, at attention, and aim his right arm with his hand formed in a salute, declaring to the object of his ire, "I know umma go to jail, but um gone kill you." To my knowledge, he never killed any of his charges.

Sgt. Moyeta, Mexican, also a Vietnam War Veteran, was always serious business. I might have seen him smile once. However, it was a good idea to be just as serious as he was when he was around. One day, our whole platoon was being punished in the pits (large area of sand that makes exercising harder), when Pvt. Knight, a black recruit from Detroit, Michigan, threw some sand in my face while we were performing an exercise on the ground. I threw sand right back at him, but I got caught.

I Love America But America Don't Love Me

Sgt. Moyeta instantly ordered me to the front of the group, and to stand at attention. He said, "Look at these silly bitches, laugh at them, laugh at them." And for the first time since I'd been in boot camp, I laughed hysterically, until I heard a voice from the pits. Pvt. Forrest, a white recruit from West Virginia with a strong southern accent yelled, "Byirt, you son of a bitch."

I instantly stopped laughing, snapped back to attention and focused on Pvt. Forrester. I stood there at attention until the pit punishment was over. As soon as we got to the barracks, I caught Forrester in the stairwell and hit him in the jaw for calling my mom a bitch, But Sgt. Moyeta saw me do it, and raced up the flight of stairs, ordered me to attention and hit me in the solar plex, seemingly with all his might. My knees buckled and I bent over. He ordered me back to attention and I re-assumed the position, until I was dismissed

Sgt. Watson was our 4th drill instructor and the one who we preferred the most. He was only hard on us when he had to be. Time was less stressful when he was in charge.

Training consisted of a lot of exercise and Marine Corps history, combat maneuvers, man-to-man, hand-to-hand combat training and water survival training. It was in Water Survival Training in which Private Knight, from Detroit who had earned the reputation as a Bully was found out. To be qualified in water survival skills, you had to be able to tread water in the deep end of the pool for an hour and turn your shirt into a flotation device while doing so. On the first day of Water Survival Training, everybody was told to jump in the pool, and everybody did, except Pvt. Knight. Upon seeing Knight still standing on deck, one of the drill instructors asked him why he had disobeyed orders and not jumped in. He started to cry, and with tears in his eyes, he replied, "Sir, Sir the private can't swim Sir."

It took all of four drill instructors to throw him in the shallow end of the pool as he frantically resisted. When they threw him in, it seemed as if in a single bound, he jumped back on deck, crying harder, "Sir, Sir, Sir, the private can't swim Sir."

After Pvt. Knight's display of fear at poolside, even the smallest recruits wolfed back at him because they saw he was basically harmless and needed not to be feared.

Boot camp also included qualifying with the M-16 rifle. A quote that we were taught goes something like this, "There are many rifles like this, but this one is mine, don't call it a gun because a gun is between your legs and meant for having fun." I didn't have any shooting skills. The only weapon I had ever used was a BB gun. But I did manage to qualify as a marksman, the lowest qualification level. Later in my enlistment, I did learn to shoot, and I did qualify as an expert.

During the two weeks at Edson's Rifle Range, a big fight broke out when while standing in formation waiting for our drill instructor to come march us to the chow hall, a drill instructor for Battalion 1102 decided to march his battalion through our platoon. I was near the front of the formation when I heard a commotion and looked back. Platoon 1102 was half-way through our ranks. I immediately turned, ran back, and delivered a double kick with my right foot, landing directly under the chin of the first attacker I could get to. I saw Pvt. Silva, a recruit from New York, Pvt. Murray from Cleveland, throwing hands and kicking too. When the smoke cleared, my home boy Barry was still geared up and yelling, "Don't nobody fuck with my platoon," while he was being held back.

Away from the confusion, the recruit who I caught under the chin, wandered aimlessly about in pain. He had to have his jaws wired shut. We were being taught that Battalion 1101 was a family, and all I was doing was defending my family. After I did it, I felt bad. But no one ever pointed the finger at me for this deed, and training went on as usual.

Each training battalion was made up of four platoons that competed against each other in various competitions throughout boot camp. I was the pugil stick (prop for a rifle) Champ for the 1st Battalion recruit graduating on Jan 9th, 1974.

I didn't realize it at the time, but we had been subject to a bit of brainwashing. We were told things like, once a Marine, we right there with God. Even when it rained, the rain was supposed to fall around us, we couldn't get wet. And some of us believed it.

I don't remember the date, but with about three to four weeks left in boot camp, Art and I received word that our friend Himey, who had received a basketball and baseball scholarship to the University of Wisconsin at Superior, had died mysteriously. In the end, his death was attributed to a bit of food acid going down the wrong pipe while he was on the court at basketball practice. I took the news hard and our drill instructor gave me and Art the option of going to his funeral. But that option meant that we would have to start boot camp all over again upon our return. So, we didn't attend Himeys' funeral which was supposed to be the next day when we found out. Later it used to break my heart whenever I saw his Mom and Dad and they started to cry when they saw me. Neither one of them lived long after. They both died early from Broken Hearts, his father especially because he saw some doors that had been closed to him open for Himey only to be taken away so abruptly. He simply lost his will to live and I could see it in his eyes whenever we would meet.

Near the end of boot camp, we were all called to the classroom, (the floor in the barracks around the Duty Drill Instructor's desk) We were all told which field and what place each of us would be reporting to for our Military Occupational Specialty (MOS) training. Throughout boot camp, I'd learned that many of my comrades, both black and white, had been given a choice of enlisting in the Corps or going to jail. Now all of us who made it through boot camp were being set on career paths in various fields.

In my eyes, one of the few things that our recruiters told us that didn't turn out to be a lie, was that I received my requested MOS, and was being assigned to Administrative School in

I Love America But America Don't Love Me

Oceanside, CA at Camp Delmar. Staff Sgt. Bryant complimented me in his unique way, while trying not to show me favor or his softer side by saying, "Son you might look big and stupid, but you obviously got smarts." In the battery of tests that we took upon entrance into the Marine Corps, my combat and administrative scores were my two highest, tied at 107. I don't know how they did it, but they read me right.

Art liked music and music equipment. So, his guarantee to attend Communications School was honored. After his 10-day leave from boot camp, he returned to San Diego for his specialty training.

Barry didn't ask for an MOS guarantee and therefore was assigned to combat school as an 0311, military rifleman, also known as a grunt. After his 10 day leave from boot camp, he went from Infantry Training School in San Onofre, California directly to Saigon, Vietnam, and he was there when America evacuated and left South Vietnam in a bad way. January 9, 1974 was the last day that I ever laid eyes on Barry, but I heard he made it home.

Friendships had formed and there were a few guys in our platoon who were from the Los Angeles area, and a lot of us made plans to go to LA for a couple of days since it was right up the road.

But when the Commanding Officer said "Dismiss", we all shot out in different directions heading home.

When I got home to my mothers' door, I knocked and she looked out at me and asked, "who is it." She did not recognize me. My lil afro was gone, and my mannerisms had changed, which she later said was much to her delight.

When my 10-day leave was over, I reported to Administrative School at Camp Delmar in Oceanside, California, and found that there were about six of us there who had graduated boot camp together. While at Camp Delmar, we had freedom and were free to go and come as we pleased, as long as we made it to class on time and completed our assignments in the barracks, the base jail and supply, both in the same building where I did my chores apart from school.

Camp Delmar was the home for Amtrak's, as well as Admin School, and was located on a beach on the Pacific Ocean. One day, a group of us were returning from liberty in San Diego and walking near the Amtrak Complex when I saw two guys from my platoon in boot camp who I knew. They were on guard duty and I decided to approach them. When I got near the guys, they acted like they didn't

know me and assumed the position of port arms, saying, "Halt, who

goes there." I kept walking towards them as I replied, "Y'all know

me." But when I got closer, they got more forceful, so I jumped in

the air doing my double kick and broke one of the guard's M-16 in

half. My other friend locked and loaded on me, so I threw my hands

in the air, turned around, and walked back to catch up with the

friends I'd been hanging out with.

No sooner had we gotten back to our barracks, it seemed like

a whole Platoon of 21 Area Guards were there intending to arrest

everybody who I was with. But I immediately told them that I was

the one who had broken the M-16 and that I was the only one who

had entered the restricted area around the Amtrak Complex. I was

locked up overnight in the same jail where I did my military chores

and wondered how some of the guys got there. The next morning, I

was brought in front of the Officer in charge for an Article 15

violation. I was found guilty and fined $125.00.

I left the hearing, went across the hall from the Officer-In-

Charge's (OIC) office to the head, entered a stall, and cried like a

baby. The Officer that dropped the fine on me came in and heard me sobbing. He appeared to be touched by my pain and asked me if it hurt that bad. I managed to yell out a, "Sir, yes Sir.". He couldn't understand that $125.00, (in today's money is about $700.00) could be life changing for me because I had a baby boy to provide for. The fact that I had something taken from me that I couldn't fight about, worried me too. The Officer didn't say anything else. He handled his business and left. After I pulled myself together, I left $125.00 lighter.

A few days later, I was called to the OIC's office. Investigators were there from San Diego to question me about Sergeant Moyeta. They asked what I knew about the fight at the rifle range between Platoons 1101 and 1102. My first thought was that they were coming to punish me for my part in the fight. But what they wanted instead was witnesses to testify in a Court Martial trial in San Diego against Sergeant Moyeta. I told them that I didn't know anything bad that I could tell or testify to. I didn't have no ill will toward Sergeant Moyeta. I remembered that we were family and chalked up boot camp to me becoming a better man. I managed to survive the $125.00 loss and I graduated from Admin School on time, near the top of the class.

I Love America But America Don't Love Me

CHAPTER 5

Upon completion of Admin School, I received orders to report to Company A, 8th Engineer Battalion, Force Troops Complex, Camp Lejeune, North Carolina, a place I'd never been and assigned to a unit in which I knew no one. I was assigned to Company A, Admin Office as an administrative clerk and drew an extra assignment, "Company Education and Training NCO," even though I was just a Private. I was also assigned as the Company Mailman.

Leon Spinks, a heavyweight Boxer who would go on to win a split decision in a bout with the greatest, "Muhammad Ali" to become the heavyweight champion of the world in 1978, was

66

stationed in the 5th Area at Camp Lejeune. I ran into him on the base three or four times. Later, I learned that his job in the Marine Corps was simply to train and box for the Marine Corps' boxing team.

Housing was different at Camp Lejeune in the Force Troops Complex. Instead of living in an open squad bay, everyone lived in rooms designed for four people. I was assigned to a room with a Mexican Marine named Jose Lima's, and two white Marines, whose names, I can't remember.

For the first week or so, I went out and explored the town of Jacksonville, North Carolina every night, trying to learn the city while grasping the fact that I was really out here in the world on my own where I didn't know anybody.

Usually, when I got back to my room, I would flip on the light switch long enough to see how to put the numbers in my combination padlock to my locker, then I would quickly turn off the light. On this night when I entered the room and felt for the switch, I couldn't feel it. A voice in the room coming from PFC Babner's direction said, "Don't you turn on that light, Nigger." Finally realizing that the light switch had been covered with tape, I quickly managed to rip it off, flip on the switch, and without a word, headed towards Babner's bunk and started dropping them B's on him while he tried to cover up and avoid the pain. The duty NCO and some others heard the commotion and rushed into our room, pulling me away from Babner. The duty NCO asked, "What Happened?" I responded, "He called me a Nigger." And before I could get the words all the way out of my mouth, he said the magic word again, "Anybody act like you is a Nigger." And like a scene from the Hulk, I broke their grips on me and hit him in the jaw one more time before they grabbed me again.

That night the duty NCO, who was also white, wrote Babner up for initiating the confrontation by taping up the light switch and verbally assaulting me when he called me a nigger.

The next morning, the top Master Sergeant Baflin (E-8) dropped the charges against Babner and charged me with assault on a superior, PFC Babner. At my Article 15 hearing, I was fined $125.00 again. It hurt me bad and cut me deep, but I didn't cry this time. I thought about it, two months in a row, $125.00 loss. At this rate, I'll never have enough money to feed or be able to take care of my baby boy properly.

I Love America But America Don't Love Me

I knew in my heart that the first $125.00 was my own stupidity. But this time, it just wasn't right. I never would have hit Babner if he hadn't call me a nigger. I guess that was okay. I thought about it long and hard and came to the conclusion that if I was going to experience success in the United States Marine Corps, and not have them take back $125.00 dollars every month, then I had better learn to turn the other cheek, recognize and put in to play that old saying, 'sticks and stones may break my bones, but words will never hurt me.' I realized at that point that I couldn't let anybody 'beat me for my cool' because it might cost me another $125.00. and I was determined to take care of my little man. After they took that second $125.00, everything was calculated.

Jose Lima's, my Mexican room mate who was from Chicago, and was gone most of the time, but had been in and out the room, and hadn't paid much attention to me before the incident. One day, he asked me where I was from and I told him that I was from Rockford, IL. "Aaah man, you my homie." And from there, we developed a friendship that still lasts.

Soon after that though, birds of a feather started flocking together, and more friendships were formed. There was Smitty, who was from New York; Quick was from Baltimore; Brother Hall, I forgot where he was from; and Bro Robert Earl Sims, the worldliest one of us all, who was from Wilmington, Delaware. After all these years later, I can still hear him saying, "Eddie 'C,' if you see something you want, you got to put your foot on it, put in your application, there's a fifty/fifty chance from the word go, you never know, they might be thinking the same way you thinking."

Another friend was Eugene Blackmon from Memphis, Tennessee. One time, Eugene faced an Article 15 hearing and lost. He came to me and asked me to write up his appeal. He gave me all the details and I wrote and neatly typed two or three heartfelt pages, and he won his appeal. I believe what clinched it for him, though was he added his own hand-written appeal on a sheet of notebook paper that was from his heart, telling the power that had he been trained like I had, his appeal would look like the one I had written. But he hadn't been and proclaimed his innocence in his own heartfelt letter. Like I said, we won.

I was performing my job admirably and receiving top scores in all areas, except conduct, due to the two Article 15s when it was time for promotions. First Sergeant Roone asked for a waiver on the trouble that found me, and I received my first stripe on time.

Later in the year, it was A Company's turn to rotate to Camp Garcia, on Vieques, Puerto Rico. Vieques was a small island set apart from the main island. A Company would be there for about four months, because the 8th Engineer Battalion was sent there to construct roads on the island. Somehow, the trip from Onslow Beach, North Carolina to Vieques took four days by ship. We spent most of our four days practicing general quarters, cleaning our living areas, and playing cards. Jose gave me a little Spanish translation book intended for greetings and other small talk and tutored and tested me on my progress on all four days that we were aboard the ship.

When we finally arrived, we were told, without reason that we wouldn't be allowed to go in the town for the first two or three weeks. Unfortunately, we had arrived during monsoon season and it rained for two weeks, seemingly non-stop. It was during those times that I was introduced to the game of chess, sometimes called the game of life. It took me about four years to win a game, but I finally mastered the game and began to be able to apply some of Chess' concepts to everyday life. Everyone should learn to play.

I Love America But America Don't Love Me

When the base restriction ended, Jose was the only one in A Company who had already seen the town. He had "illegally" borrowed a horse and kept it in one of the abandoned Quonset Huts on the base.

During my first night in the town, I was shocked to see that some Puerto Ricans were darker than me and had nappier hair. We went into a cafe called the Pirates' Den, where on sight, a pretty caramel-colored Puerto Rican waitress came up to me and said, "You a fine black man. If you stay here, you going to be mine." I'd recently gotten married to my high school sweetie, and I just had to resist temptation. The usual route to town was what they call 6 by military trucks, with seats facing on the back of the big truck. The last truck headed back to the base usually left town around midnight, and mostly everyone, except for Jose, was usually on that last truck.

One day, while performing my administrative duties, Sergeant Fitzgerald, A Company's Admin Chief, brought me the draft of a letter to type. The letter was requesting a meritorious promotion for Combat Engineer, PFC White to become a Lance Corporal. I took the letter to 1st Sergeant Roone and pointed out to him that all the scores used to justify PFC White's meritorious promotion, except conduct, were all below my scores. He asked, "So you think you deserve a promotion too?" I told him, "Sir yes Sir," even though the extra 'Sirs' aren't necessary after boot camp. Anyway, he told me to type a letter for myself as well. I did and we both were promoted meritoriously to Lance Corporal. 1st Sergeant Roone who was a white man was a very fair man.

During my time at Camp Garcia, Lieutenant Colonel McKenzie, white and permanent personnel started a football team, and I decided to join. Unlike in high school, I got to stand up. I played offensive end and defensive cornerback because that's what our team needed in a year that should have been my sophomore year in college. About four other guys, including Jose from my company, tried out and made the team. The league was made up of military bases and small colleges on or near the main island.

Even as a first-year team, we were better and much more physical than most of the teams who we played against. Our team consisted of quite a few good, experienced players who were steered to join the Marine Corps. Tragedy struck in a home game though. I was the gunner on the punt team when I raced down field toward the punt returner who hadn't signaled for a fair catch, and I basically ran over him at full speed, while tackling him. He got up and trotted off the field but collapsed at the sideline. A little while later in the game, a Medivac helicopter came to transport him to a hospital on the main island. I had no evil intentions. I was just playing hard like I'd learned to play. I didn't know any other way!

Our next game was the following week on the main island at the Naval Base, Roosevelt Roads. Minutes before the game, Colonel McKenzie approached us and told us that the injured player from last week's game had just died.

On the first defensive play of the game we played that day, as I made a tackle, pain shot through my whole body. I felt paralyzed for a second or two. But as quickly as the pain had come, it left. I didn't even have to miss a play. I felt like God talked to me though but didn't fully understand the message and I counted my blessings. I attributed it to inferior equipment and the possibility of a pre-existing condition. It happened within the rules of the game. I don't know if the Marine Corps or anybody else ever did anything for the man's family who had died. But I never heard anything else about the incident. My team mates never talked about it that I know. The only person that ever said they noticed a change in me was my Mom.

I Love America But America Don't Love Me

Only one team had managed to beat us when the time came for A Company to rotate back to Camp Lejeune and make way for B Company. Me and the others on the team from A Company stayed on at Camp Garcia in order to complete the season. We managed to earn a spot in the Championship game that was rumored to be being played on TV in the States, and everybody looked forward to it. When the season was over, Colonel McKenzie told me that since I'd just gotten married in June, that I could go home to Camp Lejeune and return with my wife and baby boy to attend the Championship Game that was to be played in two to three weeks. With that in mind, I chose home. But the other company members stayed.

To get back to the states, I flew on a C-130 cargo plane. The seats on the plane were on both sides facing each other, with cargo space in between. The ride was scary because the bumpy ride felt like and sounded like a big raggedy bus. We made a pit stop in Guantanamo Bay, Cuba before finally arriving at the Marine Corps Air Station in Beaufort, South Carolina where we got a bus back to Camp Lejeune and life before heading to Puerto Rico.

About a week before the big game, the Captain called me into his office to let me know that I had orders to report back to

Camp Garcia, Vieques, but that I didn't have to go. I was disappointed because the coach, Colonel McKenzie had told me that I could bring my family back with me. Looking back, I think that the Colonel was a good man, and I believe that if it was in his power, he would have stood true to his word. But for that reason, and my hesitancy of riding in a plane that rode like a bus, I decided not to go back.

When my teammates from the company returned, I learned that they had won the championship game without me and had avenged our one loss that season.

Later that year, a celebrity of sorts joined our unit. It was Gunnery Sergeant, Johnnie Ashe, the younger brother of tennis great Arthur Ashe. For anybody who don't know the story, Johnnie had volunteered for military service and Vietnam so that his brother could pursue his championships without the threat of having his tennis career interrupted.

CHAPTER 6

As the second-year anniversary of my enlistment approached, I found out that I could reenlist, adding two years to the three years I had originally committed to, be promoted to Corporal, and receive a $1,300.00 reenlistment bonus. I was 20 years old and had never had $1,300.00 in my hand all at once, so I re-upped. In today's money, that $1,300.00 would be the equivalent to about $6,200.00.

My reenlistment also required that I change duty stations. First, I was reassigned to 2nd Bridge Company, 8th Engineer Battalion. But instead of the staying in the Force Troops Complex, I was assigned to Camp Geiger, located on the other side of Jacksonville, North Carolina.

I Love America But America Don't Love Me

On my first day at Camp Geiger, I ran into one of my drill instructors from boot camp, Sergeant Moyeta. But now, Sergeant Moyeta was a Lance Corporal. As a fresh and newly promoted Corporal, I now out ranked him. The man had been to war and fought for us. I had nothing but admiration and respect for Sergeant Moyeta because he played a major part in turning boys to men. Some of those men just found it hard to handle.

A few weeks later, I received orders to report to the Marine Corps Development and Education Command at Quantico, Virginia where Marine Corps Officers and Federal Bureau of Investigation agents receive their training. Upon arrival, I was supposed to be assigned to the Classified Control Center, but I couldn't start work before I received a Top-Secret Security Clearance. In my past, I had created a paper trail, and the incident with the beer prevented my approval for a Top-Secret Clearance. My paperwork was denied, and I was approved instead for a Secret Clearance, due to the trouble I got in when I was only 17 years old. Subsequently, I was assigned to a Company Office.

When I arrived at Quantico, I'd just missed the last football season that the Marine Corps would play on the big stage. I ran into

Billy Lewis, a star halfback from my alma mater who had already graduated when I got to Rockford West. He was about to receive awards for his performance during that season.

Quantico was still a great duty though. The nation's capital was about 30 miles away. It was there around 14th and T streets where for the first time I saw and recognized, on a large scale, a lot of people who had gotten lost in their dreams, and many who never dared to dream at all. In the Corps though, I had a great job and a great Admin Chief, Gunnery Sergeant Robert L. Davis who was White. Sgt. Davis saw fit to promote me meritoriously to Sergeant. My primary function was as a Separations Clerk and later I earned a Second Military Occupational Specialty (MOS) as a Career Planner. Having obviously performed both jobs with expertise, I received the meritorious promotion. For a Marine to re-enlist or leave the service, they had to see me.

During my 2 years and 11 months in this capacity, I was relegated to intramural flag football, fast-pitch softball, and I was the leading scorer on the battalion basketball team in a league of 9 to 10 teams. I averaged about 26 points a game with all my points coming down low and a whole lot of rebounds. The term most people used for my leaping ability was, "phenomenal for a man my height."

While also at Quantico, I took in some of the sights and visited a couple places where major Civil War Battles took place. The Battle of Fredericksburg took place right outside the back gate at Quantico. And the Battle of Manassas took place a few miles northwest of Quantico. I found it to be so amazing that so many Bible-toting, so called Christians, would fight and die for an institution as evil as slavery. I also found comfort in the fact that so many people were also willing to fight and die against this type of evil.

Currently my best weapon against this type of evil was my vote. I was at Quantico when I jumped in my car to ride all the way to Rockford, IL to vote in my first presidential election ever, for President Jimmy Carter.

I developed strong friendships with two white men at Quantico, and if I could say anything to them today, it would be, "Gunnery Sergeant Davis and Staff Sergeant Viar, I love you guys, because of the little trials and tribulations we went through together, and because even though y'all out-ranked me, y'all treated me with respect and as your equal." And y'all was there for me, a time or two for all 2 years and 11 Months. "I salute you two because my race didn't matter to y'all." Gunny was a teammate on the basketball team as well as my Admin Chief, and he always stayed cool and calm and kept it real. Staff Sgt. Viar was a little wiry fellow who fought in Vietnam. He was also my flag football teammate who would always playfully declare that he would whoop my big ass if I got down wrong. Peace and Love to you both.

As I went about my routine and doing my job, I counted down to the day of my discharge. I was liked and respected by my peers and everyone who I met, until the arrival of my second Commanding Officer at Quantico. He was a white Captain out of Louisiana who came to the company under fire and was facing a Court Martial for handcuffing a black Marine to a bunk to ensure his presence for a move aboard a ship for a cruise, and other civil rights violations at his previous duty station.

I got a feeling about him quite like I imagined James Brazier from Dawson, GA might have been feeling when he was scorned for being able to afford nice things and drive a new car. I have no idea what I did to this man. He didn't have a problem with how I performed my job or with my behavior. But still, just didn't care for me and had his ways of letting me know.

On my last fitness report (exit report), and after giving me excellent marks in every category, he wrote, "Sergeant Byirt, in his capacity as Separations Clerk, has been entirely dependable and an asset to this command's administration, up to the date of his detachment to terminal leave status. His work has been without error, on time, and there literally has never been a problem with separations under his tenure. That is a significant achievement and speaks highly for the Marine's integrity. On the other hand, Sergeant Byirt did not care to contribute much as an NCO during this period. He anxiously awaited the beginning of his terminal leave and was a classic example of a "short timer." He remained congenial and effective administratively, but matter of factly, took off his pack in all other endeavors, became a clock watcher and on the side, contributed his expertise as quarterback to the Battalion football team." A copy of my exit report follows:

I'm sure that it was Gunny Davis who gave me the excellent grades. But the Captain couldn't let me leave without his remarks. It probably would have killed him to allow me to depart without chopping me down one more time. I was ready to go, and he made saying goodbye to the Corps easy for me.

CHAPTER 7

Fresh out of the United States Marine Corps with job skills and an Honorable Discharge, my old Boss at the Metal Treating Plant, let me know that my old job was mine if I still wanted it! However, I had big ideas about where my career was headed and pay from the plant was not going to be enough. Besides to Mr. Charlie, I was a Nigger, but now I had options. My intentions were to find a great paying job in the field that I'd took courses and worked in the previous 5 years and eventually get my own business.

My Job Search began at the Employment Office where I found out that, outside of having a High School Diploma, Affirmative Action was in effect and a Campaign, "Your Best Bet is

I Love America But America Don't Love Me

to Hire a Vet", was supposed to be working for me.

After about 3 weeks, no jobs in my chosen and preferred field became available, but United Parcel Service (UPS) called so I went to work for Big Brown as a Delivery Driver even though I'd never drove a 5 speed stick shift in my life or a truck that big.

Having only been with UPS for about 3 weeks, I had an accident two weeks in a row. In the first one, it happened on a Monday, I backed into another truck that was parked next to the space that I was trying to park in to make my delivery. As soon as I jumped out of the UPS truck to inspect the damages, there was an old man who heard the bump, coming to investigate. I reported to him that everything was okay and that there was no major damage. However, he saw different. We went inside his little shipping office and we called my Supervisor to let him know what happened. My Supervisor was cool about it and told me to finish my delivery there and to carry on.

I almost made it through the next week without incident, but that Friday, it happened. I pulled up to a factory named Weyerhaeuser on Rockford's East Side to make my delivery, but when I got to the back of the truck, the door was standing wide open and the biggest package on the truck that day which was meant to be delivered there, was missing. I jumped back in the truck and headed back to my previous delivery location. As I approached, I saw the package laying on the ground right where my truck had been parked. "Thank You, Thank You Jesus", I repeated to myself several times. I picked up the large parcel, put it back in the truck, this time closed the door, jumped back in the truck and sped back toward Weyerhaeuser. Upon arrival this time, I was driving too fast for conditions trying to make up for lost time. When I hit their Parking Lot, Big Brown just started sliding on the ice. I couldn't stop and was heading toward a row of parked cars. I thought it was best to try and steer through the gap that separated the two sections of the employee parking lot but, I didn't quite make it. I slammed into a car in the front row on the left side and pushed in into two other cars behind it. When I got out to survey the damage, oddly enough, it seemed like no one had seen or heard the accident and the foolish thought of not reporting it flashed in my mind, but I looked at Big Brown and there was major damage and a head light was hanging down.

I Love America But America Don't Love Me

I went inside and made the dreaded call. This time, the Supervisor told me to wait right there. He sent 3 men in three trucks. Two of them split the rest of my route up and the 3rd one took me back to the Delivery Center where I received my last check signifying the end of my United Parcel Service Career.

The United States Postal Service, NI Gas, the electric company, water company all called not more than a month later, but on Feb 12th, 1979, I became Rockford, Illinois' 5th Black Mailman in a city with a population of 144,000, 13% Black. According to those statistics there should have been at least 21 more of us. It took about 2 more years before Rockford would hire it's 6th Black Mail Man, Wayne Mims.

The 1st day of delivery was the coldest day in my life, temperature wise! I wore some jeans, a shirt, a short leather jacket, combat boots, with a couple pair military issue green wool socks, military issue black leather gloves and the first thing the Post Office gives letter carriers depending on the season that you start, a Winter Cap in my case with the ear flaps.

I felt like all eyes were own me as I prepared to hit the streets and I was confident that I was being talked about by some of the other carriers. Nobody said anything then, but later, I found out most of the conversation was about how poorly I was dressed for such a cold, cold day.

On the route that 1st day, I was so cold that I was trying to hold a handful of letters between my thumb and index finger and managed to drop a big bundle of mail just a couple stops into a long swing, prolonging my time in the Freezing temperature, because I had to put the mail back in sequence before I could continue delivering. Never thought about throwing in all in the bag and going back to the truck.

After I got off work, that night, I went and bought Ski-mobile Coat, Ski-mobile boots, Ski-mobile mittens that went all the way to the elbow, a Ski-mask, a couple pair of Long Johns and some more cotton socks. Even though I grew up there, when it was cold, I was in and out. Never dreamed of working in it. That day was the beginning to my learning how to sweat in double digit below zero weather.

Opportunities in my chosen field still hadn't become available but I still had hopes of working in a business type environment so when registration for courses at Rock Valley Jr.

I Love America But America Don't Love Me

College came around, I took advantage of the G. I. Bill and enrolled.
I went to work full time daily, school by night and still found time
for recreation ball.

For whatever reason, I became a target for Disciplinary
Action. One day 3 Supervisors followed me to lunch for which I
was allowed 30 minutes plus two, 10-minute breaks while on the
streets. At the time I didn't know they were hiding outside of this
restaurant where a few carriers always went for lunch. When I left
after my 30 minutes, I didn't know that they were following me.

After a couple stops on the route, I took my first 10-minute
break where I always did on this particular route which was at a
friends' house that I knew from High School. I don't know how long
they followed me that day but when I got back to the Post Office, I
was informed that I was facing disciplinary action for taking an
unauthorized break that went over 1 minute. Instead of applying
what I believe is now called Progressive Disciplinary Action they
went after a weeks' pay off the rip. I filed a grievance with the
National Association of Letter Carriers' Union and got all my money
except overtime.

Things at the Post Office kept going south. The next incident

I Love America But America Don't Love Me

happened One day out on the outskirts of Rockford's far South side, at a "Whites Only" trailer park that I had no idea was there while I was growing up. Any way as I made it down the little snow-covered dirt road, I could see some folks standing around and about and assumed they were waiting on the mail. The mailboxes were on poles in groups of about 5 or 6 in each section. When I go to 3rd or 4th section, a middle-aged man took exception to a Black Man delivering his mail. Even though it was cold outside and snow on the ground several people were gathered near and around his trailer as he stood in the door and decided to alert the others, "Look e here, I'll just be damn, a Mother Fucking Nigger delivering the damn Mail." I threw the Mail Jeep in park, at the same time reaching back for the snow chains while at the same time he saying, to his old lady who was standing just behind him in the doorway, "Baby hand me my .357 magnum", and in an instance he had it in his hand, saying, "Jump on down Nnnnnigger, with your Black Ass so I can light your ass up with my .357 " Needless to say, I decided not to put the snow chains up against the .357 magnum. I was mad and shook up, but I swallowed the insult and kept delivering the mail.

When I got back to the Post Office that day and told my

Supervisors about what had happened, they told me not to worry about it and chalked it up to maybe the man had had one too many drinks.

One day the next week, I was assigned to the same route again but there was hardly anybody if any waiting for the Mailman. And I wondered was I riding into some type of trap or set up. They had to have been told that I was going to be the Mailman that day. When I got to the mailboxes in the group that belonged to the gentleman who threatened me with his .357 and called me a Nigger, I put a sales paper in everyone's box but his.

When I got back to the Post Office that evening, I found that I was facing disciplinary action for not delivering this persons' junk mail sales paper and could get a two-week suspension for it. I filed another grievance with the Union, and I was exonerated. Had it been a first-class letter, the outcome may have been different. This time, though, Management had to sign a letter written by the Union that said in part, "Mr. Byirt shall be treated fairly and equitable along with all other employees in the Future. But it was only a piece of paper. Guess who got the longest walking route with the most mail all the time.

I Love America But America Don't Love Me

I was treated differently in terms of positive awards as well. On this particular day, I was only 2 or 3 deliveries into the day delivering mail on South Main right after the left off Harrison when a middle aged White Lady came running frantically from the back of her house crying, "Please come, Help me, Please help me." I threw the mail truck in park and ran following her back to the rear of the house. When I got back there, I heard an elderly White Man moaning and saw that the car that he was under had slipped off the jack in a way that it couldn't be re-used and that he couldn't move. I quickly tried to lift the car off him, but I couldn't. Hearing the lady still crying, I took off back to the street to get more help. I quickly got another Black Man who was passing by in his Job Truck to stop and we both ran back and tried to lift the car off the old man. Both of us together couldn't, so he took off back to the street for even more help.

The man had quit making noises when his daughter let out a deep, pitiful and wailing sound of urgency when God gave me the strength, I tried again and lifted the car off of him held it until the old man was pulled from underneath.

92

I Love America But America Don't Love Me

I didn't stick around to see what happened next. I immediately went back to delivering mail. Later that night I learned that the incident was newsworthy and that all 3 of Rockford's TV stations and the newspaper had come to the scene and reported it, but I wasn't there. I was long gone when they arrived. I didn't want to give the Supervisors no more reasons to mess with me. They had me on the run.

I wasn't looking for any accolades from the Post Office, but I knew that some had been given for similar deeds. Examples can still be found in the NALC Magazine.

In the streets, right place, wrong time January 9, 1981, the 7th anniversary of my graduation from Marine Corps Boot Camp became the coldest day in my life up until then, but it wasn't because of the temperature. I'm glad they didn't kill me. Thank God for just a couple of witnesses. No less than 8 Officers of the Law beat and kicked my Black Ass, then tried to blend my head in with the concrete once I was down. I was thinking that no, this can't be. I was a United States Marine Corps Veteran and a current United States Postal Service Letter Carrier, and I hadn't done anything but be Black.

I Love America But America Don't Love Me

That New Year's Eve, a White Police Officer had been killed by a Black Man so in the aftermath the RPD gathered up like packs of wild dogs, ran wild, went on a rampage actually, kicked and beat Brothers asses for at least a solid month. Like I said before, it took them until the 9th to get me and I had to stand trial for getting my ass beat.

Attorney Samuel L Dean (RIP), the only Black Attorney in town at the time was my Lawyer and at one point in my trial the Judge told him to "shut up". The only word missing was "boy," but the contempt was there. Anyway, when the smoke cleared, I had a record for damage to the police car because I tried to kick my way out. My reason for being in the car in the first place was irrelevant.

Football wasn't completely out my blood so when news spread that someone in Rockford was bringing the semi-pro team, the Rockford Rams back, I got a rush. When the time came, I tried out and got a starting Line Backer Job. A few of the players on the team had played some in college and most played in the Big Nine and surrounding areas.

We lost our first game which was a home game against the Delavan, Wisconsin Red Devils 35-7. I got our 7 on a forced fumble recovery and run back 66 yards. I also had an interception and recorded 14 tackles. A lengthy article titled, "Rams Be Deviled 35-7," covering the game with a still picture of me in pursuit was in the paper the next day so I gathered up all the newspapers I could find. When I got back to work, I had a few fans and I autographed some copies for my co-workers. The Rams didn't have much of a team that year. I scored a couple more defensive touchdowns and was tied for the team's leading scorer halfway through the season.

I worked, played football, recreational Basketball and went to school until I earned my 1st associate degree. It was in General Business Administration. A year later, I received my second Associates Degree, this one in Business Management. A 4 yr. Degree wasn't readily able to be obtained in Rockford at that time.

One day shortly after I'd gotten the second degree, I was looking at the Post Office bulletin board and saw that a Personnel Assistant Job had become available. I automatically thought the job was mine and applied for it.

However, the job went to a young White girl who had only graduated from high school about 6 months earlier. At the inception of this book, she had made it to the Head of Human Resources at the

I Love America But America Don't Love Me

Rockford, Illinois Post Office. From my understanding she's now recently retired.

The color of my skin cost me another opportunity at a job in a field in which I had worked in for 5 years in the USMC, earned two Meritorious Promotions and had received two Associates Degrees.

I filed an Equal Employment Opportunity complaint. The Post Office has its' own EEO office for Rockford, based in Chicago. I tried some private attorneys, but the usual answer was that my money wasn't long enough to battle with Uncle Sam and that a case like this could run into years.

Any way the Post Office EEO resolution was for her to keep the job and use me as a 204B (Supervisor Training) in situations preparing me for the position of Carrier Supervisor. Over a period of the next few months, on occasion, I got to wear a shirt and tie and play temporary Letter Carrier Boss.

Somehow it came to the point when all the regular supervisors except Billy Bowens was trying and inventing new ways to sabotage my Postal Career. A strange turn of events occurred when a large amount of Cocaine and a pistol was dropped in one of

96

the Big Blue Collection Mailboxes that I was supposed to pick up had I worked that day.

Coincidently, I had called in sick but the discovery of the drugs and gun that the replacement carrier found in my absence became newsworthy on TV and the newspaper when he reported his findings. Under pressure from his peers to do me dirty, Billy Bowens gave up his Supervisor job and went back to carrying mail.

Later, EEO ruled that in keeping up with Affirmative Action, the Rockford, Illinois Post Office had to have a Black Carrier Supervisor. A population of 144,000 people, and the United States Post Office in Rockford, Illinois had never had one. Again, I figured that the job had to be mine. I'd done a lot of fighting and had the credentials but instead the job went to the 6th Black Man to carry mail in Rockford, Illinois. It was a friend from High School, a fellow Warrior and a friend that I still hang with whenever we're in the same town.

At one point though I felt like he should refuse the job and step aside for me. But who does that? He came too to my house and asked me to fill out his Postal Service form 991 and help him do the paperwork necessary for his promotion and I did. Together, we both knew that, though I was the one who had did all the fighting, the powers that be at the Rockford Post Office would rather be damned to hell than have me reap any of the fruits of my labor. I was hurt when I didn't get the job but felt a bit of pleasure with my Friends success. Now at least we had one. At one point, he told me that he felt like he was being put in a position to fail so he decided to tighten up long enough to retire as a U.S. Postal Service Letter Carrier Supervisor.

Realizing at that point that I wasn't going to be allowed any upward movement within Rockford's Postal Service, I went back to school and got my Real Estate License. To my knowledge Rockford didn't have any Black Real Estate Agents at that time. I continued to carry mail and dealt with the Real Estate part time but found more pain there.

Another fellow postal employee that traveled and hung out in the same circle of friends as I, a West High Grad and Warrior Alumni allowed a White Mail Handler who also had his Real Estate License to reap the benefits on the purchase of his home, the same one he lives in today, some 30 plus years later. My friend wasn't the one to tell me though. It was his White co-worker who approached me with a s--- eating grin on his face smiling from ear to ear, " Did you hear, I just sold your boy a house."   I was shocked and hurt but to this day, I've never said a word to him about it even though we have mutual friends and have been in each other's company many times since. I thought first of all with us both being Black, both West High Alumni, both having roots in Rockford's West End and us occasionally running in the same pack, that I would be the one to sale him a house whenever he decided to buy one, but he taught me some valuable lesson, that it isn't always about the Brotherhood with everybody, sometimes other factors come into play and a Man do what he want to do with his money.

With assistance from the Veterans' Administration, I who had mostly came up on Rockford's south side bought a 4 Family apartment building on North Avenue on Rockford's north side where few Black Folks lived at the time. Three of the apartments in the building were already occupied when I moved in. One apartment was occupied by a White classmate from West High, his wife and child, another by his mother and the other one by a large heavy set, middle aged white male.

He didn't even give it a month. Within the first two weeks, my classmate gave me his thirty day notice, taking the time to tell me that he wasn't moving because I bought the building but that he'd been planning to move even before, but just now had at last found the right place. A couple weeks later, his Mom gave me her notice. It was still hard for me to grasp this Racism thing and to what its extent it goes, so I did a little soul searching regarding my business and personal life and found my way to Rockford's biggest church which was at least 96% White. I paid my tithes and attended faithfully.

The vacancies that I had were filled, 1st by a friend and the second by a single Italian Lady with a young daughter. After she'd been there about a month, her biggest complaint was that there was no washer or dryer in the building. She asked if she could hook up her own in the only place in the buildings' basement set up for a washer and dryer. I told her she could if everybody else in the building could use it. She came back instantly asking me, "Have you lost your mind?"

I mulled and prayed about the situation. One day shortly after, while sitting in the break room at the Post Office, I decided to look in the classified section for washers and dryers. Lo and behold, there was a coin operated set for sale. The price for both was a hundred and seventy-five dollars. I took my money out to count it and BAM, I had exactly $175.00. God looked out for me again. I bought the set and before long, I got the $175.00 back plus as they became another small source of income. I felt like God sheds his light on me because I was a good man and tried hard all the time to do the right things. However, the landlord business also gave me a firsthand lesson along the subject of "Not doing business with your Friends."

The church that I was attending offered counseling on various matters. As I was trying to get my life together and get some understanding, I sought counseling. One of the White female counselors at the church told me that, "If God's got something better than Sex, he must be keeping it for himself", when I told her that my only vice at the time was Sex.

Later, the Pastor of the Church made the Rockford News and was forced out after tearfully and publicly confessing his sins for Adultery and other misdeeds. I eventually found my way back home to the church that I grew up in where my Mother attended faithfully and my Great Uncle Albert and Great Aunt Frances were ministers,

The House of God Church.

CHAPTER 8

The next Football team that I played for was the Rockford Panthers about 2, 3 years after the   Rams. That team had talent from Chicago come to play in Rockford and had Rockford's own J-One Love, a young, shut down, Pro material cornerback who never went to college and later joined the U. S. Marine Corps. With me and him on the same side of the field, opposing teams got nothing on our side. Together we played a big part for our team in a Semi-Pro Superbowl, Victory somewhere in Nebraska where I played indoors the only time in my life.

After a particularly good game I was interviewed by a local television sports news reporter. When I got to the party, several people there started telling me that they had just seen me on TV. I felt like a Ghetto Superstar. The next day I was able to see the interview myself and I liked what I saw, Geri Curl and all.

In a game later on in the season, I came from my Linebacker spot from the Defensive Right on a Blitz untouched with the Quarterback posing like the Statue of Liberty, with his back to me looking down field to his right for a receiver to come open. It was a maim shot for sure, but I pulled up. I tackled him forcing a fumble that we recovered but my teammates, Black and White got real upset with me. One of them reminded me that it was just like Chess, "If you eliminate the Queen, the game is over." I never told any of them that I had played in a game where a man had died as a result of his injuries. It wasn't something that I was proud of. I can't say if that was in the fore front of my mind, but I did pull up. I was older then and I couldn't see maiming that man in a game for $35 or $40 dollars if we were lucky enough to get it. Like I said before though we were good enough to win a Semi-Pro Super Bowl that year.

The following February came and some of the guys on the Football Team, Kaspar, (The Ghost), Blake, (RIP) another Marine Corps Vet, the fastest man I ever laid eyes on, the Newton Boys,

I Love America But America Don't Love Me

Chris and Carl, another Marine Corps Vet and Captain Steel Bill Sanders who went on to become Rockford's first Black High School Head Football Coach and others all got excited because the 1st National Football League Combine was being held in Indianapolis, Indiana and anybody who thought they had skills could supposedly attend and tryout.

I requested time off from the Post Office to go but was denied and threatened with the loss of my job if I went. I thought about going anyway, but I came back to earth and thought about my 6 kids by now and how they depended on me. Another opportunity denied. I thought to ask, since there was so much hate and disdain for me in the air and they don't want me around, why not let me go in hopes of me being successful in my endeavors. I couldn't understand their efforts to keep me around and concluded that some folks just need punching bags to boost their feelings of superiority and some are just truly possessed by the Devil!

Several of my teammates and friends did go to the combine but only Ghost was signed. He was one of the fastest men at the combine, but he had stone hands, so the San Diego Chargers sent him back to Rockford after about a month in Camp. Carl Newton was a big power back and his brother Chris who had played football in college at Northern Michigan was fast and the best Wide Receiver I ever saw up close and personal were both good enough and I couldn't understand how Chris didn't make it because he had a shot in college. None of the others had been to college, which I believe was unwritten protocol to play in the NFL back then but waived for that first combine in Indianapolis if my memory serves me correct. The truth of the matter is that a few of us were good enough to play in the NFL. Our misfortune was coming up in Rockford oppressed and where the ceiling for success was low and success for us was joining one of the Military Services then getting out, coming back, finding a job and avoiding jail. Even though Chicago, Milwaukee and opportunities were only about 90 miles away, it was hard for the lot of us to see that far until it was too late.

CHAPTER 9

In 1988, a transfer request that I'd made to the Atlanta, Georgia Post Office two years earlier finally came through. When it did come, I was torn between staying or going two years later but I was born in Georgia and had heard about all of the great strides that African Americans had made in Atlanta and I wanted to be a part of the progress being made.

I made the move in June and when pay day came, it was just like clockwork. My check was there so I didn't miss a beat.

The atmosphere and moods within the Postal Service in Atlanta was a lot different than Rockford. I was assigned to the Hapeville Branch out near the main Atlanta Airport and on the same street as the Ford Manufacturing Plant at the time. All my Supervisors were Black and probably 70% of the Clerks and Carriers. Even before I got there, the city of Hapeville had earned the nick-named, "HATEville" by some African Americans due to acts of Racism directed at them by some of the towns people in the beginning.

While in the office preparing mail to go out on the street, every morning, somehow an agreement had been reached when I got there where we would listen to a Black Radio Station for perhaps 10 minutes and then a White Radio Station for the same length of time and this went on for the duration of our Office Prep time.

On my first day of delivery, I encountered Culture Shock when I walked into a tall, multi-story, Brand New Building that housed the M&M Hair Products and saw that everybody in there was Black. Big Business in Rockford was Boxes' Barbeque in a small one-story building on Marchesno Drive. I thought to myself that, "Yes. Atlanta got to be a Black Mans' Heaven. C

Coming from where I'd been. I thought that here, I'd surely be able to move on up.

I visited the Doctor King Memorial and other sites honoring

I Love America But America Don't Love Me

the Civil Rights Movement taking advantage and gaining knowledge

about some things that were foreign to me coming from Rockford,

Illinois.

The first night that I went out on the town in Atlanta, I met

Tommy Lister, aka Deebo at Dominique's Club downtown on

Peachtree. At the time, I couldn't think of his name, so I asked him

about the Football Show on HBO that he had a regular part in.

Needless to say, he was happy to claim the fame. And I rubbed

elbows with the Big Dog and his entourage. When the Fire

Marshall's came through and shut it down, he invited me to continue

to party and ride out in the Limo with his entourage that had several

lovely ladies. I would have been one of no more than 3 or 4 guys. I

was tempted but, I declined his invitation. I was just an old country

boy from Rockford always on guard and didn't want to get out my

lane. I couldn't leave my car and security because at the time, I just

didn't know enough about Atlanta.

At the Post Office, it wasn't long before another form of hate

showed it's ugly and unsuspecting head. The Post Office in Atlanta

had a Softball league, so I joined the Hapeville Branch Softball

Team and through conversation learned that one of my teammates was from Chicago and was in middle management at the Main Post Office on Crown Road. When I told him that I grew up in Rockford, he was warm to the Midwest connection. I told him about some of the things that I went through at the Post Office in Rockford and about some of my hopes and aspirations. He told me that he was pretty sure that he could start me on my way and to come see him in his office at the Big House.

When I went to visit him, entry into the building provided more surprises. The work force appeared to be mixed 50/50. When I got up to the top floor, it was less activity, but while walking along the hallway looking for my Midwest Connections Office, I noticed that up there the mix was more like 90/10 or 85/15 in favor of Whites.

I made it to my friends' office where we chatted a bit and he told me that he would talk to his Boss and have him call my Boss to get the ball rolling on a possible opportunity for me.

A couple of days later he called me to tell me that his Boss had made the call, but instead of talking to a Real Supervisor, he talked to a member of the "MoreTeaSir" tribe who was what they call a Career 204B in training and trying to climb himself. A

110

supposed to be Black Man did me dirty. He told the man with the power to lift me, the man with the power to give me what I'd been chasing, the reason that I came to Atlanta, that I wasn't serious about my job and paid too much attention to the ladies. My Advancement went from 100 to 0 in the span of a telephone conversation with a delusional, self-hating, Black Man. In affect I was Black Balled in Atlanta before the 1st year past.

Needless to say, I was surprised and hurt by this turn of events, but I never confronted the man or voiced my displeasure to him about his assessment of me to a Man that held keys for my progression in his hands.

Over a period, I found that I was resented by some Blacks as well as Whites and was taught the difference between a Yankee and a Damn Yankee. "A Yankee may come to visit, but a Damn Yankee comes to stay." After a while I was able to form the opinion that a lot of the people at the post office acted like crabs in a bucket, pulling others down so they could climb up, Black and White. That trait may be unwritten protocol for the job. If you show you'll shit on your buddy, you in the house!

I Love America But America Don't Love Me

A few months later the man that gave the bad report on me, who was probably in his late 30s', early 40s' got so gravely ill that he had to retire from the Post Office. Shortly, after his retirement, by chance I ran into him on the streets and he looked sick and like a man who had aged 30 Years in a matter of months. He eventually passed at an early age.

A few days later an African Preacher whom I felt like was sane and serious about his business, at a Church near Gilbert Gardens Housing Project in the Poole Creek Neighborhood gave me a perspective that I'd never considered before. During my first and only visit there, when I walked in the door, the preacher proclaimed that I was, "The Chosen One" and said to me in the middle of Church, "You don't need no Guns or Knives, you don't have to lay a hand on nobody, you the Chosen one and God got you!" I wondered if that was the case, why did I keep coming up on the short end and what could I possibly be chosen for.

It was at the Archives at the age of thirty-something when and where I learned that 1870 was the first year that Negroes was on the United States Census by name instead of property and up until 1865 Negroes were just 3/5 of a person and depending on the number of slaves helped establish Voting Power. Can you picture that. Somebodies did. What a creation. 3/5 of a person.

I had always been curious about my sir name and its' origin when I found out about the Archives Building on Capitol Avenue in Downtown Atlanta at that time. Every city that I'd ever been to, had no Byirts' in the Phone Book, unless they were close relatives that I already knew. Once I even paid for a heritage search. They sent me a small leaflet back that had info on my Mother who was really a Crumbley and a couple of girl cousins that I knew about in Jacksonville, Florida. That was it.

Through research at the archives and Latter-Day Saints records via his wife, I met a white cousin who was the Great-Great Grandson of my Great-Great Grandfather J. J. Crumbleys' sister. His wife was warm to me and excited about the connection, but he was indifferent. I delivered mail to a white Mr. Crumbley that was a spitting image of my beloved Great Uncle Albert who was Black. Just recently, I met a younger cousin from the same tree on his job. We chatted a bit and he seemed to have accepted the facts. Now whenever I see him, it's like what's up cuz and we're cool with that. To hate a Crumbley would be to hate myself because, in the words

I Love America But America Don't Love Me

of Football Great Terrell Owens, "I love me some me."

I know through my Genealogical Research that there seems to be a concerted effort even now by most of the White Crumbleys to keep the past in the shadows and that some have gone through great lengths toward that objective. Another partial line from the Jadakiss song "Why" says, "We don't need the accolades, just the acknowledgment." I'd bet at a Family Reunion that everybody would be pleasantly surprised by the similarity's even though we share different skin tones. I say to the Crumbleys, let's put this Family Reunion together and be an example for the United States of America.

Back to the Atlanta Post Office, obstacles and tests were still being placed before me, but then all my Bosses were Black, but not all were bad. The first incident that comes to mind is when I happened along a large amount of cash stuffed inside of an envelope inside of a mailbox at house that I was making a delivery to. I knocked on the door, but no one was home. I retrieved the envelope without ever counting the money for its safety and when I got back to the Post Office that evening, I turned it in. Milton Howard, my supervisor and a couple of friends Lucius Boddie, Carlos Banks, both Letter Carriers all teased me about turning the money in and said that the Station Manager was keeping the money for himself. I didn't hear anything else about it until I asked Mr. Willis who was the Station Manager at Hapeville at the time passed through the West End Station where I was working then, and I asked him what ever happened to it. He replied, "Son it's a good thing you didn't take the bait." He said it was a set up. The week after I found the envelope, on the same route, I pulled up to a mailbox down the street and around the corner and there was a 100-dollar bill just lying there on the ground a few feet away. Guess what happened to that hundred.

On another occasion, I found a .45 Caliber Pistol in one of the big Blue Collection Mailboxes at the corner of South Side Industrial Parkway and Jonesboro Road. I didn't bother to touch it but instead called my Supervisor. Supposedly, it had been stolen from the Fort Gillem, Army Base a few miles up the road.

Shortly after that incident is when I transferred to the West End Branch Post Office. In the West End I saw a lot of people who got lost in their dreams, but I also saw a lot of people managing their business and living their Dream. At the Post office it was still mess though and before long, I got a 2 weeks suspension when I was charged with not picking up 3 test letters on time from one of the Collection Boxes at 2001 Martin Luther King Drive. The evidence was that 1 test letter came back post marked a day late and supposedly the other two, 2 days late, without being post marked. The 2 weeks suspension was worth at least a $1000.00 in lost pay, but I went to the Labor Pool and worked both weeks for pennies. When I got my Post Office pay stub, I saw 0s' across the board. I wrote "Thank You, Mr. Hayes." on it and went and placed it on his desk.

I filed a grievance with the National Association of Letter Carriers Union, but Management took it all the way to arbitration. The Union President for the Atlanta Branch at the time was a Black Man, a Reverend, got in touch with me to tell me not to come to the Arbitration Hearing. He told me that I was going to get a weeks' pay back and that "We" were going to give Management a week. I let him know that that didn't sit well with me because I was not guilty.

On the day of the hearing, I put my suit and tie on and showed up anyway only to have the reverend angrily approach me, admonishing me for coming. One of the Arbitrators', a White Gentleman overheard the exchange between me and the Union President. When the President left, the Arbitrator approached and asked me if I felt that strongly about my innocence. I assured him that I did. He told me not to worry and that I would get both weeks' pay back, minus overtime. He stayed true to his words and I did get my money back, no thanks to the Union President who hung me out to dry. I just couldn't understand how he could compromise on my innocence.

Around this time, I was reading the paper one day and saw where the Falcons' had signed Clay Matthews who was about the same age as me. My wheels started turning and I thought that this might be what the Preacher was talking about that day in church when he told me that, I was the Chosen One. I entertained the thought; might it still be my calling to play in the National Football League at my age. I was still physically gifted and had recently been lifting weights for the first time in my life for appearance and playing a lot of Basketball to stay in shape. But with that news, I worked out harder and into the greatest physical condition that I'd ever been and got stronger than I'd ever been at any time in my life including Marine Corps Boot Camp. Then I recorded a video of myself bench pressing 225 lbs. twenty something times, turning some flips, performing other acrobatic moves, hanging on the Basketball Rim and sent it to the Atlanta Falcons requesting a try out.

Over a period, I sent a video to all the National Football League teams in the Southeast, plus the Minnesota Vikings and Philadelphia Eagles because they had Black Coaches. Maybe I thought too much of my Marine Corps and Government Service. I was denied via first class mail by all, but no one bothered to tell me that they thought I was crazy.

Around October of 1995 word spread about the Million Man March called by Minister Louis Farrakhan and oh, how I wanted to be in that number but when I requested the time off, I was denied and told that if I went any way, I wouldn't have a job when I got back. I think one of my faults, but also a strength at times in my life is that I've always played it safe. Anyway, I didn't go. When I heard about the beauty and the love shared among the Brothers from all walks of life, I felt inspired and hate I missed it.

I Love America But America Don't Love Me

Meanwhile, at the Post Office with my Black Supervisors, there was more mess and other small grievances from time to time but basically smooth sailing, as

long as I stayed in my place and didn't try to move up within. I earned the nick name "Ed Sanford" on the job when I bought an old Blue, long bed pickup truck and was seen scrapping on my off days. Living in Atlanta was expensive because there was so much to see and do.

The next unforgettable experience that I had in Atlanta was away from the Post Office when I saw Evander Holifield walking through the Airport between fights Tyson I and Tyson II", before Mike got some ear. When I realized that it was him, I started walking after him calling his name, "Holifield, Holifield." After about the 4th or 5th Holifield, he stopped and turned around with a stone cold look on his face that made me think I might have to defend myself against the Heavyweight Champ of the World or run, but ain't no scared bone in my body especially man on man because I know David slew Goliath and something I got from a Cowboy flick many years ago, "It ain't a horse that can't be rode or a man that can't be throwed. Anyway, I extended my hand and told him that I just wanted to shake his hand. He shook my hand, turned right back around and walked away without ever saying a word. I stood there for a minute dumbfound and looking at my hand wondering what had just happened. An older Black Male Airport Employee, who had witnessed the interaction stood there shaking his head and said, "Something ain't right with him," a black female employee wasn't as nice, she said, "I'm surprised that M. F. stopped." Later, I told my friend Walter Cummings from Detroit about what happened. He told me that he never would have approached Holifield because he was a Man just like him. But Holifield was a hero to me and I guess that's one of the differences in growing up in Detroit versus small time Rockford. I gathered from that experience that Holifield must have felt the same (just a man) and I found out once again that with a lot of folks, it ain't about the Brotherhood at all, sometimes Folks might not want to be bothered.

At any rate, I still admired Holifield and though not quite as Star Struck, am proud of him for his accomplishments in the Ring at his size. He exemplified the saying, "It ain't the size of the dog in the fight, it's the size of the fight in the dog."

I Love America But America Don't Love Me

Thanks to tickets won on V-103 from DJ Portia Fox to a P Diddy Album release party at the Velvet Room. I rubbed elbows with the likes of Magic Johnson, Jason (JET), Jermaine Dupree, others and had a Ball. Just like the first time I rubbed elbows with the stars, as soon as the host, this time P. Diddy said he was going to buy the bar, the Fire Marshalls came through and shut the party down.

Some years later I paid $250.00 and was finally able to see my first Professional Boxing Match. It was Lewis vs Tyson in Memphis, Tennessee. Even though my ticket cost $250., I sat about 7, 8 rows from Ringside when I found a seat where no one sat and didn't come to make me move. After the fight, I felt sorry for Mike because no way could I have wiped sweat from the man's brow after he had just got done whooping my ass and then sitting up talking about how he had to discipline me. No! No way.

At the Post Office I had long ago given up the fight for advancement within. A few more years passed me by and after changing Branches a couple of times I came to the last one on my postal career the Ralph McGill in the little five points area where the great and generous philanthropist Tyler Perry first studio was. I came under the command of Station Manager Lela Greene, a damn

Yankee from New York whose aunt who was also a transplant but the Postmaster of all of Atlanta. I had found that the Atlanta Post Office was an Industry becoming dominated with Black Females in Management Positions. My theory was that in trying to meet numbers established by Affirmative Action, they got two for one, a Black and a Female thereby pushing Black Males further down the Food Chain. I thought back about Slavery days when some of the Sisters could get out the sun and in the house with the master. It's sad but they are in so many cases Societies greatest weapon against Black Males. This lady became the greatest threat to my Postal Career. She was a tall and somewhat attractive, but for whatever reason, she'd often find the time to leave her office and come to the workroom floor, harass me and try to make me Bow down. That thought crossed my mind, but she was also Married to a gentleman in Management at the Post Office. After all my years at the Post Office, she found fault with just about anything I did after having done it well over 25 years. More and more, I found myself in fight or flight situations with her. Ever since that day when they took that 2nd $125 back in boot camp and I had resolved to not let anybody beat me for my cool, but she got oh so close on several occasions.

I Love America But America Don't Love Me

Because I had been diagnosed with stress and hypertension bad enough to get put on the Family Medical Leave Act (FMLA), 3-4 days a couple times a month, I flew on numerous occasions much to her dismay.

. Things got so bad that I had to file several grievances and complaints against her. I wrote her bosses and other individuals within the Postal Service that I thought might be able to help with my situation to no avail. I finally wrote Georgia Congressman Johnnie Isaksen a Republican several times. He went to bat for me, mainly on the strength that I was a Veteran. My letters resulted in a big conference between Management and Labor and her easing up on me. I was so grateful for his support that when Congressman Isaksen's time for re-election came, I crossed party lines for the first and only time ever and voted for the Honorable Mr. Isaksen. He did me a solid and earned my vote. However, I voted Democratic on the rest of the ticket including President Obama for his first term.

There was a rule at the Post Office that employees, not talk politics on the job. However, leading up to the election everybody talked politics. Within the station I found that individuals were divided along racial lines even though our Union had endorsed the

I Love America But America Don't Love Me

Democratic Party.

Because of how I was raised and what I'd seen, I thought to myself and out loud that there was no way possible a Black Man could be elected President in these United States. I was sure he would be assassinated before America would allow that to happen. Then it happened and I became even more worried that the President was still not out of the woods.

One of my white co-workers whom I considered a friend, who I'd been talking politics with and who voted Republican declared to me after the election that President Obama was just as much his President as my President because the Presidents Mother is White. Indications led me to believe that the reason he voted against President Obama was because his Father was Black. My friend and co-worker decided to agree to disagree on some subjects and moved on and remain friends.

I languished further at the Post Office until the day of my 55th Birthday. The system had beat me down. While out on the route that day, I turned to reach for a package behind me in the delivery truck and pain shot through my back and down my right leg. At that moment, I considered my 5 Years in the United States

I Love America But America Don't Love Me

Marine Corps and 31 Years with the United States Postal Service, and now that I was old enough, I had just delivered my last piece of mail. I drove back to the Post Office, parked the truck, took the keys to my supervisor, told her that the truck was outside with mail in it and I left, never to return.

I had a few months of Sick Leave that they're supposed to add on to your service time if you don't use it and was near Maximum Vacation time for which Retirees usually get paid for at retirement, resulting in a 5 figure send off.

To prepare you for what came next, I'll lead with a quote from a play by William Congreve, "Heaven has no Rage like love to hatred turn'd/Nor hell a fury like a woman scorn'd."

After requesting my official retirement, something that usually took about 30 days, I sat home waiting and waiting and waiting, using up my sick leave. A couple more months went by and I heard nothing. Finally one day, I got on the phone and made enough calls to learn that my Retirement had already been approved, but was being held up because, even though requested more than once, they were waiting on necessary paperwork from the Station Manager, the same one who had a part in the decision I made to

125

retire when I did.

Another month or so past and I ran out of Sick leave, so I started using regular vacation time in order to keep getting my bi-weekly check. That became a state of emergency, so I wrote Georgia Senator Johnnie Isaksen again and again he came to my aid and got the ball rolling, Finally, after all of the ignored requests from the Office of Personnel Management to my Station Manager and after she'd delayed my retirement long enough to use all Sick Leave and Annual Leave, I finally received my Official Retirement for 36 years of Government Service.

If it doesn't sound like you, then you shouldn't be offended but in the case of my Station Manager and others, our Black Women are the systems greatest weapon against the Black Man. I don't know what I did to her. She came into my life, punched me right on out the door and delayed my official retirement nearly 9 months and robbed me for my nest egg. As we all know some at the Post Office have not left as quietly.

After retiring and having laid around for a few months doing absolutely nothing but watching TV, eating and waiting on the Electronic Funds Transfer (EFT), I got an E-mail from the Veterans'

I Love America But America Don't Love Me

Administration introducing a Veterans Retraining Assistance Program (VRAP). There was another EFT involved so I applied and was accepted. Next, I had to be accepted at a college that would be approved. I chose Atlanta Metropolitan State College.

Atlanta Metro offered two majors that was eligible for the program. One was Business Administration and the other Criminal Justice. I already had two Associates in Business, so I chose Criminal Justice and graduated with honors.

I entertained the thought of starting a new career and seeking a job in the field on the oppressed side. Ultimately, I chose not to. I figured that my Retirement Pay supplemented with some Rental Property and strict Management, I could survive.

Content to finally be able to pay all my bills on time and save a few dollars monthly for my Grandkids, I figured I'd just fade off into the sunset and then 45 happened.

CHAPTER 10

Homage to the GPOAT

It was then 2016. The Presidential Election Campaign and events starring 45 kept me glued to CNN. I'd never watched the political events and happenings as close until then. 45 lifted the ratings for all the major media networks. He was in the discussion of children as young as 9 and 10 years' old. He captured everybody's attention.

The more I watched and learned about him, I thought surely that this person who was born with a silver spoon in his mouth and they say got his 1st million to get started from his daddy, ain't a Real Man. He had shown all the signs and characteristics of an Anti-Christ and a Demagogue. I figured that no way on earth could he be

I Love America But America Don't Love Me

President of the Most Powerful Nation on Earth, the United States of America. On the world stage, I wondered if a new Hitler was in the making.

He was Racist, a divider, suspected drug addict, suspected pedophile and the biggest liar to ever take a dump between two shoes. I couldn't believe that America would even allow a clown the platform that he stood upon, let alone campaign for President.

Finally, there it was, confirmation of what the Preacher in Church meant when he said I was the chosen one. Because I love America, even though America don't love me, I felt a call to action.

How could this happen America? YES, this was my calling, to help shine the light on the absence of moral character in so many people and on the ugly mark against our country and the religions practiced call Racism and White Supremacy.

If for telling the truth as I've experienced it and see it and it lead to more bad Luck for me, perhaps I will become a Martyr, but not in the way of the two young Black Veterans who made the news for their actions in Baton Rouge, Louisiana and Dallas, Texas. I want to live and experience the Love.

Those young Black Men, Military Veterans both trained and

made in the United States of America was I suspect, confused and delusional and because of their confusion and delusion committed horrible atrocities against America. Haunted by the lives taken by them in the name of America, they couldn't get past the fact that they're friends, their neighbors, their cousins and other innocent young black men were being shot down in the same streets that they had killed to protect. Imagine their confusion. Every time I hear about another person killed in the streets by those whose job is to serve and protect, I just cry!

During his campaign 45 brought the hate out, made it popular for some people to smack certain other people "upside the head, to punch them out and said he would pay their legal fees. He cried build a Wall to keep the Mexicans out, ban the Muslims and preached a message of division and hate, while never passing on an opportunity to claim that he was the best at everything. He even claimed that he could shoot someone down in the Streets of New York and no one would say anything. I detected crazy and evil and felt like anybody that lined up with this evil would be Hell Bound too.

Daily news kept coming out as the media dug into the

candidates' past. When news came out that 45 had been sued and lost in Civil Court during the 70s' for Racial Discrimination, I figured he'd lost any chance at a Black Vote. He wouldn't show his taxes like every candidate had in the past and that meant he was hiding something from the American people, the people that he wanted to lead. Then the people found out that he wasn't such a great Businessman and that he'd lost close to a billion dollars in one year. We also learned that he hadn't done like every other U.S. Citizens and some foreigners in some instances paid any taxes in almost 20 years. Nor had he contributed one thin dime out of his billions to the Military or Veterans Association. He in fact went to extra ordinary measures to avoid being drafted into Military Service. If he hadn't claimed that near billion lost on his taxes that we got to see, I'm sure America could have used that cash on a much more worthy cause. So far, he'd set a great example for the people he wanted to lead.

He claimed that Hillary Clinton was pay to play and pocketing contributions to the Clinton Foundation, however there was never any proof of that. But when the people looked at 45s' Foundation, they found evidence of personal spending for items such

131

as a Large Painting of 45 himself. They found a contribution to an organization in Florida that was about to investigate some of his dealings that ironically stopped after a donation from his foundation. That sounded like pay to play to me. I thought that everyone would be able to see the crook in that. Everything that he accused Mrs. Clinton of, he already knew because he was already guilty himself. An update: His Charity was shut down for impropriety.

The American people heard about some of the stories in which poor, small time subcontractors and other small business were hired by 45 that he refused to pay and left bearing the weight of his debt while he escaped by declaring Bankruptcy at least 6 times. One of his favorite sayings was that he was smart because he uses other peoples' money and to me, that sounded just like a Pimp.

During the campaign, a tape came out and 45 is bragging about assaulting females and being able to grab them by the Pussy and get away with it because he was rich and famous. Many Americans thought that would be the final nail in his coffin regarding his run for President.

We also wondered why 45 would not say anything negative about Russia's Dictator. Just about everybody knew that 45 owed the Bank of China, owned by the Chinese Government somewhere around $650,000,000 but wondered, what was the connection to Russia. Fast Forward to 2019 and leaks regarding the possibility of A Tower in Moscow finally hinted at the answer.

In the first Presidential Debate, the one that the sniffles were so evident in, 45 asked Russia to hack Hillary Clinton' e-mail server and more e-mail started pouring in. As they came in, they only provided more fodder for 45s' movement. I thought to myself that, perhaps there was a possible strike against Mrs. Clinton maybe two, but during the campaign, 45 had given the people samples of all 7 of the Deadly Sins. Pride, Greed, Lust, Gluttony, Wrath, Sloth and Envy The signs were all there.

Late in the Campaign things were going well for Mrs. Clinton and she was enjoying a double-digit lead in the polls after winning all 3 debates. She had even started campaigning down ballot when Juliano appeared on TV boasting about a Bombshell that would turn the race around in favor of 45.

Within the next day or so, the FBI Director went against his bosses' recommendations and protocol, sent a letter only to the GOP at first and announced that they were investigating more of Mrs.

Clinton's e-mail.

Almost immediately the polls started to shift in 45s' favor, as he fed his crowds lies such as , "If Hillary wins, she'll be tied up in court for years, doing a dis-service to the American people," leading the people to believe that she wouldn't be able to focus on her duties as President of the United States.

What he didn't tell the people, was that he himself was already facing at least 75 lawsuits and that one of them was allegedly regarding a thirteen-year-old girl losing her virginity.

The FBI Director did indeed drop the Bombshell that Juliano forecast and later denied. They left the lie out there for 9 days during the height of early voting and the polls spiraled downward for Mrs. Clinton. After the ninth day Comey came out and said that there was nothing new regarding the e-mail investigation, but a lot of damage had already been done. Millions of people had gone to the polls believing that Hillary Clinton was going to jail. For 9 days the lie floated. After wards, the American People learned that the new investigation could have been conducted in 9 hours. It didn't take 9 days. In my eyes, it was crystal clear to see that Assange (WikiLeaks), Russia, Juliano and the FBI Director colluded to change the course of the election.

In my opinion, the DNC panicked and didn't need to focus as hard as they did on the Black, Hispanic and other vote. I felt like they should have concentrated more on the White people on the fence. In truth it seemed like Mrs. Clinton forgot about some folks or either took them for granted.

I am a big fan of the Obamas, Beyoncé, Jay Z, Lebron and all of the others celebrities that made appearances in support of Mrs. Clinton like most African Americans, but 45 had brought out the hate and their appearances and success just provided more fuel for hate like James Brazier and so many others in Dawson, Ga, my birth place, felt by what turned out to be enough of the American People to put the Devil himself in the White House. With his election, in the words of Gill Scott Heron, it was truly, "Winter in America."

These people had absolutely no interest at all in having a White Woman carrying on President Obama's Legacy. For them, his legacy was a nightmare and they didn't want any part of it or anybody to do with it. In my opinion President Obama served all the people well.

45s' hate message gave his supporters a voice because he said the things that they obviously wanted to hear. Around Atlanta, signs supporting 45 were less evident but a different story in Dawson Georgia. Signs were rampant. It was as if the people that support 45 silently said, "let's go get the most vile and immoral person on the planet and make him President of the United States of America.

Clearly, America was a better place while President Obama reigned but there was no way that many People, who can't kill the seeds of Racism within themselves, allow a white female to carry on the legacy of a successful Black Man. They'd be damn to Hell rather than allow it. And hell is what they chose. 45 showed us all 7 of the deadly sins but prevailed.

1. His **PRIDE** was evident and on display when coming down the stairs to announce his run for President for the whole world to see long before he decided to tun for Office.

2. **GREED** was shown by the fact that, even though he claimed to be a Billionaire he still needed the title of President in order to complete him. I wondered if he's donating any part of his salary to a worthwhile cause like I've heard of other Presidents doing.

3. **LUST** had been witnessed by him needing three wives, his

alleged affairs while with them, his taped conversation with Billy Bush and the gang of Women who got together from different parts of the world to tell lies on him.

4. It was just pure **ENVY** that he showed for President Obama, starting with the Birth Certificate. The results of the election reflected an air of Envy by 45 followers as well.

5. **WRATH** toward anybody that saw things differently or said anything against him was displayed via twitter.

6. **SLOTH** was clearly present. Just look at his past. He never did a hard days' work in his life and in fact stood on his Daddy's shoulders with a one-million-dollar loan to get started in business. Self-made Man, no way!

7. **GLUTTONY** was evidenced by his love for McDonald's and the weight he gained since he started on the Campaign Trail.

One sin not listed among the deadly sins is **LYING**. It happens daily several times. Last I heard he had told over 16,000 documented lies and still counting. America showed it true color. With 45s' election, America said, screw Black Folks, we don't love you and don't care if he did discriminate against you and wouldn't let y'all in his Whites' Only Apartments. America said screw the

I Love America But America Don't Love Me

Muslims, "you're all terrorist and we don't want y'all here. America said screw the Mexicans. Y'all going to build a wall and pay for it, then we going to send some of you back then lock y'all out.

His display of the same mentality that allowed Hitler to exist in Germany and Slavery to exist in this country of immigrants from all parts of the planet is good for America in that most of the cards are on the table. And because they are, let's straighten it out. "Yes, we Can".

When he talked about Making America Great Again, he could have given the American Economy a big boost just by bringing some of those businesses overseas that make his product home. Or was he talking about times in the 17 and 1800s' when White Men ran the true Native Americans off their land and then claimed it as their own by placing a stake in the ground. I was a forty something year old man when I learned about the Trail of Tears. I don't know the name of the Warrior(s) whose blood still runs through my veins, but we still here, just trying to get some Love and live the American Dream.

When he spoke about Making America Great Again, was he talking about times when Negroes were only counted as 3/5 of a person or times like James Braziers suffered in Dawson, Georgia or Bloody Sunday in Alabama or times like the riots in Detroit, Michigan, Watts in California and other cities across the country.

Am I amazed at all of 45s' supporters, No, I'm not! I am disgusted with his African American Supporters. The most despicable human being on earth is a step n fetch it Uncle Tom. He/she has not learned that he/she is just as despicable to, if not more to the White Racist as he is his to Black People. Ask the young Black female that he would eventually have escorted out of the White House or that fellow in Chicago even though I believe they can redeem themselves. Other African Americans that voted and support 45, I say to you that Slavery could not have existed without the assistance of other Africans and it's clear some of their descendants are still here among us. I feel like you sold yourselves to the Devil. You can survive and live decent and respectable in the United States of America without bending over and you'll feel better about yourselves. Black Folks who didn't vote are guilty as well for putting 45 in the White House. A nonvote was a vote for him. I realized even back then, when I took that first trip from Virginia to Rockford to vote for President Carter that Our Vote is our Voice and there is Strength in Numbers. And folks died for that right. We got to vote!!

45 was and still is unfit and doesn't seem to have an ounce of a Moral Compass, so I'm on a mission to make him one and done. Every time I see him, I think about the sexual assault allegations, the denials and the lies that came after. If he had a Moral Compass and was a real man, he would take responsibility for his actions, past, present and future like real Men do. That alone is a great indicator that he's missing Man Skills. And what about the sniffles again in the debates. America might have put a junkie in the White House. And if not for the system of checks and balances he'd probably have America on the edge of Bankruptcy and would be no more than a Tyrant.

I know America has lost some Respect since President Obama left the job and that other countries and Foreign Dignitaries were laughing at US at the United Nations on TV. I would have never imagined a world leader tweeting and Lying to his people, having temper tantrums like a spoiled brat and acting the part of a clown well enough to be laughed at. These words mean a lot to me. Man, honor, integrity, kind, fair, honesty, reliable, caring, giving and trustworthy. I'm just one of many who have crossed paths with men of greatness, champions who possess these qualities and were fit to be crowned.   If every American search their hearts and be true we'll find that 45 wasn't fit and that none of these words apply to him. But coward and Liar does. He should Man up, show the American people his taxes, admit to the sexual assaults, affairs, own up to Ukraine and tell the American People why he's Putin's Puppet. I think Putin got his man in our White House. America need a real man. Americas' only! I feel like the real basic reason for 45s' success despite himself, was that his supporters were fueled in most cases by the seeds of racism, straight out hate because of color of skin. I've witnessed some good ole boys and those with good ole boy tendencies who still seethe at the mention of President Obama's name. 45 didn't pass the smell test from the beginning but enough people chose to overlook it. Look at everybody that got close to him starting with Billy Bush. They go from sugar to mess. They're falling all around him. One more hypocrisy, he said that Mexico would pay for the wall but then shuts down U. S Government when he couldn't make US pay. He talks about banning immigrants while those closest to him are immigrants too, from Germany, the same place as Adolph Hitler and I wonder if he got some Benedict Arnold in him too because of the sharing and keeping secrets with Russia. I also wonder if he's trying to let Russia in the back door via Venezuela. Now the American debt is over 22 Trillion dollars, the most of all time. The Criminal Justice System is a multi-billion-dollar business with 185 Billion spent on Mass Incarceration alone. Sorry Jigga Man, I know you say don't knock another man hustle, but the Criminal Justice hustle is a hustle, I got to knock. That's a lot of money invested in keeping us locked up. A certain element makes available all the tools needed to commit crime and a lot of us keep falling for the okey doke and making a lot of folks rich off somebody else pain, suffering and misery.

Fortunately, he hasn't been able to take America back to times like he called great again. As a country, we don't need a divider. Together we will surely stand but divided we will surely fall and may end up being colonized by Russia or some other country.

In spite of 45 and his supporters, America is still the greatest country on earth and a place where I now realize, you can be all that you want to be if you don't take no for an answer, starting young, if you know it isn't fair, fight when you know you right, Don't let anybody beat you for your cool, remember that he who angers you controls you, stay focused, keep your eyes on the objects of your desire and also remember that you catch more flies with honey than you do with vinegar. Easier said than done, but a pure heart with Love and a straight Moral Compass is what I try to practice. I don't have a hate bone in my body for people no matter who they are or where they came from. I do dislike certain ways, attitudes and actions. But my compass is straight.

I've been wronged by both Black and White, and it is my opinion that in a lot of cases, not all but a lot of those Black's that have or had the power were there due to their willingness to be extensions of Racism and corruption in efforts to keep a certain kind of Black Man down and in their places. I check daily but the scales still aren't balancing.

In my career I never did get the opportunity to play Football in front of the right people and never did get that office job but in spite of all that has happened, I feel like Charlie Wilson and the King, Atlanta Rapper TI say in their song, "I'm Blessed, I'm Blessed, I'm Blessed.

However, after taking my past and everything else into

I Love America But America Don't Love Me

consideration, along with the election of 45, I had more confirmation that, though I love America, America don't Love me.

In between the time of 45s' election and Inauguration, I went online to Change. Org. and started a petition charging 45, etc. etc. with Collusion. After a few hours, I'd gotten several signatures, but one of my friends in Rockford signed with a fake last name. I asked him why the fake name and he replied, the Mob ties that 45 had been proven to have and the possibilities of his overzealous supporters seeking revenge against those who spoke against 45. Because of his fear, I reevaluated the situation, pulled it down and instead, decided to put it in this book. A young lady that I went to school with wouldn't sign but told me not worry, that "God got us Eddie, man we survived Ronald Reagan, we can survive 45. To that end I say, Reagan was a Saint in comparison!

Whatever the case may be, the one thing 45 gets from me is my vote for "Americas' Greatest Pimp of All Times. He's used his position to make side deals. He got servants at the White House, Chauffer Driven Limousines, a detail of Secret Servicemen for protection, spent the salary of over 330 presidents at last count on Golf, mainly at his businesses, and flies anywhere he wants to on planet earth on Air Force One. And we pay for all of that. He even had us pay him for his private venues and hotels and didn't bother to stay, on at least one occasion. Big Pimping in Washington DC and he told us he was smarter than us because he uses other people's money. When America does get the chance to look at his taxes, I wouldn't be surprised if he didn't have as much money as me. To all of his supporters, He evidently see us all as his whores but, y'all got pimped and conned in the process and should be charged with Treason and accessory for crimes against The United States of America, land of the free home of the Brave. He has many times turned his back on some of the people that he used to get elected the first time. I hope nobody falls for the con in 2020. By now we should all be able to see clearly. It's 2020.

Finally, as expected, he was impeached by the House in December 2019, but in the Senate in 2020, he was backed up and protected by a cast of morally corrupt and spineless individual. If the saddest day in U. S History was not the election of 45, It must be the results of his sham impeachment trial.

I wonder how, could the people who allowed it to happen ever look at their loved ones and truthfully say they did what was right by our constitution and America. They can't, because they didn't! They did what cowards do. They hid in the heat of battle and chose to look the other way. The guy has created mischief and chaos all over the world and they continue to look the other way.

As an, everyday citizen but especially as a U.S. Marine, I don't want anybody with his characteristics leading me. I recently learned that 8 Marine Corps Generals have passed through 45s' administration and other high profile Marines including one who walked out on his State of the Union Address have shown their disapproval of his service, the chaos and disorder created at home and abroad by our commander in chief. These are true men of honor for which the Marine Corps is known, who unlike 45 answered their call to duty and laid their lives on the line for America whom we love. It's up to all of America, democrats and republicans to come together and stop Putin and 45 from fleecing the flocks here in the U. S. and abroad.

Regarding the Marines, we are Men of Honor dedicated to doing what's right by America and our constitution. In times of peril, the Marines are the first to be called to Americas defense. Could so many of us be so wrong?

146

I Love America But America Don't Love Me

I feel like I went out on a limb for bringing even more attention to some of the ills of our ways under 45 and speaking unfavorably about our leaders, but with biblical scripture Isaiah 41:10 in mind I continue forward. And once a Marine, always a Marine. In the Marine Corps, we have a saying, "Semper Fi", which means "Always Faithful" I'm not sure if the Marines that were bombed in Iraq have faith in Semper Fi due to the Commander and Chief downplaying their injuries as a result of some mess that he started with another country. In the Corps, many of us feel like if our fellow Marine, be he black, Mexican, white and so many others got a problem, then we all got a problem if their problem is legitimate! I believe that we all realize that America got a problem. As an organization, we're most often called the "Worlds' Finest". Once again, individually we're called Men of Honor. I'm proud to be a Man of Honor.

Within the Corps is a brotherhood like no other because we all went through turbulent times. It started in Viet Nam where Marines were fighting and dying for our country. A special handshake called a dap was developed. To start, it went fist over fist, my fist over his fist, he not above me, his fist over my fist, I'm not

147

above him. Fist back side to front side, I stand by your side, you stand by my side. Twice, knuckles to knuckles, I got your back, you got my back, then fist to the heart, "I mean it from the heart." 45 don't have our back. The Corps is just another tool at his disposal.

For those who seemingly allow 45 to happen, if money is their motivation and they claim Christianity, I suggest two biblical scriptures. Number 1 is 1st Timothy 6:10, "For the Love of money, is the root of all evil, which while some coveted after, they have erred from the faith and pierced themselves through with many sorrows" Number 2 is Matthew 19:24, "And again I say to you, it is easier for a camel to pass through the eye of a needle than for a rich man to enter the Kingdome of God." The money won't completely stop flowing if we do the right thing and apply empathy, love, morals, ethics and respect. Many times, it's been said, "If you are not part of the solution, then you are part of the problem. American, we can fix this. If a person got just one ethical bone in his/her body, we can't excuse the facts any longer. "The proof is in the pudding". Good, hard, working, honest folks are being denounced now and drug through the mud in the media and on twitter while 45 is setting properly convicted and sentenced criminals free.

I Love America But America Don't Love Me

I'm also sick with sorrow for the mistreatment of people of color and ashamed for my country because of the want to be tyrant at the helm, and the cold hearted, spineless individuals that allow 45 to happen. We all know the bottom line is all about him and I personally don't want to be his whore anymore. Never did!

CHAPTER 11

Subliminal Messages, White Supreme Moments Fact or Fiction

For America to truly be great Racism and the Religion of White Supremacy has got to be fixed, be done away with completely. Throughout my book I've given examples of a series of high-tech lynching's beginning at an early age of White Supreme moments as I've lived them. Since Football and the Superbowl, is the most watched Team Sports every year worldwide and so much attention is given to it, I want to use football to give my views on some Morality questions, White Supreme moments within the sport and ways to change one heart. Let's make it clear, I'm not calling anybody referred to in this chapter a White Supremacist. I am saying that in my opinion, they suffered White Supreme Moments at the time some of the decisions were made.

First up the 1985 Chicago Bears Coaches never got to sniff another Superbowl title because it was flat out immoral to give the ball to the Fridge before Walter Payton got his. He was the driving force in their charge to the Superbowl. It seemed as if somebody was worried about how bright Walter's star was going to shine, so the decision to dim the lights was made and they reaped what they sowed for the rest of their careers. If I could talk to Sweetness, I'd say don't worry I got you in my book and your light still shining bright in a lot of our eyes.

One more thing, Rickey in a dress and makeup. That was over the top too! I wondered if Rickey chose to wear that dress.

Back to Superbowl's, In Superbowl LII, we witnessed a White Supreme moment when the game began with Malcolm Butler on the sideline shedding tears after learning that he would not be going in to battle with his teammates, after being there in 95% of the teams' previous games. The Superbowl, the game that everybody who ever put on a pair of cleats dreamed about playing in. Those with the power crapped on their fans and members of the team to teach Malcolm a White Supreme message just like the Sophomore

151

I Love America But America Don't Love Me

Coach when I was 15 when he stopped me at the door and told me I couldn't even try out for His Team, even though I had always been in the top 6 on the teams that I had been allowed to try out and play for.

I wondered if 12 or 87 would have suffered the same fate. I doubt it, but whatever Malcolm did or didn't do, his punishment was much too severe. I considered the Fact that his name is Malcolm and wondered deep down if that had any bearing on the decision.

It was ironic that the same man who saved a previous Super Bowl for the Patriots was cast to the background. However, his absence in this game was magnified by the play of his replacement. Even though the Patriots (Americas Team) were heavily favored by the masses, I feel like they lost because of a White Supreme move, a lack of empathy for a past hero, lack of a moral compass and the decision to deprive a Man who'd had played his heart out all season long and had earned the right to Play & Shine.

But God don't like ugly. You see who got the MVP award. It was a Man of God, a Family Man, a Man giving God all his praises and talking about how good God is. He started the season low, on the bench, but once again Love and Pureness of Heart trumped hate and Righteousness shined. I'm going on record a step further and say it is my belief that the Philadelphia Eagles had the season they had the following year was because of the immoral decision to bench the Man that put them on the National Football League Throne.

Another White Supreme moment showed up in the Superbowl when Malcolm was the Hero. Marshawn Lynch (Beast Mode) had abided the special order to not hold his nuts on his first Touchdown but when it got late in the game, everybody was smelling victory, the Power and everybody else knew or thought that Marshawn was about to let his nuts hang all the way to the ground on a game winning Superbowl Touchdown and pay the fine. But those with the power decided that it would be better for someone else to score and that Marshawn couldn't be allowed to shine like that. He carried the ball all year long, all the way to the Superbowl but was denied carrying it that last yard. Once again. God don't like ugly. Instead the team went against what got them to that point, passed and Malcolm Butler stepped in, Super Bowl Hero. How quickly both Coaches dismissed what got them there, so they reaped what they sowed. I imagined if I was Marshawn, I'd want out of

Seattle too.

Regarding Superbowl LIII, as noted by a former NFL Pro Bowler, the MVP of the game missed the first 4 games of the season because he tested positive. Malcolm has no such history, so I wondered what if Malcolm had been white. What could he have done so bad that didn't even allow him to get in the game? Somewhere in there lies, a double standard.

Reluctantly I have to give credit where it's due and give the New England Patriots Dynasty it's due even though it began with the invention of the tuck rule and robbing Charles Woodson and the Oakland Raiders of a game changing play and a trip to the Superbowl for a chance to sit on the National Football League throne.

In regard, to the latest Superbowl, there was some people that were saying the 49ers wouldn't be in the Superbowl if Colin Kaepernick had been the Quarterback. With that being said, I can say that the 49ers might not have lost, had Kaepernick been the QB.

Along with my other views regarding past Superbowl games, I believe the issue of morality played a part in 2020's outcome. The 49ers are a great organization the I have rooted for in times past.

I Love America But America Don't Love Me

However, I think the 49ers handled the Kaepernick situation wrong and it couldn't be overshadowed with a 49er win. Kaepernick stands for a worthy cause that needs a remedy.

I feel bad for the players who put their hearts into their craft and the ills of an organization comes into play. I saw Joey Bolton, whose motor I admire, crying on the sideline with his teammates trying to console him when he knew the game was lost. He played a heck of a game and it was nothing that he did wrong to contribute to the lost. Personally, I would rather not go to the Superbowl than go and lose. It would be too bittersweet to get there and come up short regardless of the money!

The 49ers as an organization reaped, what they sowed. It is my belief that had they chose to acknowledge the truth about what Kaepernick is crusading for and chose to kneel beside him for a majestic and righteous cause the outcome would have been different.

Instead, Patrick Mahomes, a biracial man, black and white unified in one man was crowned the MVP of the 2020 Superbowl Champs.

I believe all organizations should implement morality in their strategies. In a truly moral and righteous world, it would have been magnificent to see the entire team, black and white, bottom to the top get alongside Kaepernick and deal with this scar on America. Right now, the world would be a better place.

Another 45 Supporter was denied the NFL Throne in a year that his team went 15-1, played in the Superbowl as heavy favorites and lost. They flopped straight out. It wasn't the fault of Cam Newton, nothing he could do about it. It was divine intervention and the Powers worthiness to sit on the National League Football throne.

There are 3 coaches that lost 4 Super Bowls without getting a win. I wondered why they didn't deserve the Throne and the Glow just 1 time. I'd bet without being there that every one of those losing team had crapped on a Player for someone with less skills. I believe it's a good bet that they also support 45 and share some of his beliefs, I whole heartedly believe that Justice was served with each of their losses.

I asked one of those coaches for a tryout at LB or SS 4 or 5 times, including the 1st year that the Atlanta Falcons went to the Superbowl but was denied. The Falcons had a QB on the team a year older than me. I can only imagine if they had given me a chance and I turned out to be as special as I knew I was. As fate

156

would have it, the oldest Defensive Player on the team put a cloud over the team and himself in the Spotlight the night before the game disrupting the Teams' Focus. Anybody else see the message! How hard and how much time would it have took to let a Marine Corps Vet and still a government employee at the time to come run through some drills and tell me I was crazy, too old or better yet, that I was truly gifted. It wasn't hard at all, but because I built myself up, worked hard for it and was written off as insignificant and given no consideration at all, I'm able to illustrate my point regarding ill will, the lack of Empathy and a sick Moral Compass again and reaping what you sow.

In 2017 in Kevin Byard's, coming out game, I'd never heard of him, but Eddie Jackson showed out in his game too. They both got Player of the week for defense, my specialty, not by choice. Any way there it was. I envisioned my whole name in the spotlight on the Football Field at the highest level. I asked myself was it truly my destiny to use football as the platform to expose and point out Racism and ways to correct it even further and to give honor to those that came before me. Regarding Kevin Byard, my last name, Byirt derived from Byard and Kevin's ball hawking skills, remind me of

157

me, except I played closer to the ball. I may be wrong and it would

sadden me a bit if not, but I believe that this Titan and I are

branches from the same tree and now our Grandfather Joseph can

finally get some Love, have more light shined on his people's plight

after coming to America and their quest for racial harmony through

Football, Kevin and me.

CHAPTER 12

In these last pages, I want to shine some of the light on how many of our youth that are still without proper guidance that are still being detoured and having paths impeded toward greatness, life, liberty and the pursuit of happiness. Because of White Supremacy, tons of talent have been suppressed and inferiority complexes created in towns like Dawson Georgia, my birthplace and Rockford, IL where I grew up for many, many years. To steal a line from 50 cent, there are a lot of Diamonds in the dirt, that ain't been found.

The fix must start here. It's time for folks, black, white and others to stop growing up in America scarred by Racism. Where was

I Love America But America Don't Love Me

you Eric Thomas (ET) we could have used you even more back then. In the words of Frederick Douglas, the Great Abolitionist, "It is better to build strong children than to repair broken men." Frederick Douglas also said, "I would Unite with anybody to do right and nobody to do wrong." Through the times that I've endured from childhood until this moment, I've learned that a sound Moral Compass and Mutual Respect is necessary, will eliminate problems and carry us all a long way on a righteous and moral path. I got pushed off the path early and it's taken too long to get back. Now I want to plant a forest of Empathy, Love, Moral, (ELM) trees add Ethics and Respect and have everyone practice being an ELMER. Empathy, Love, Morals, Ethics, Respect.

Fellow Americans, when you know you wrong, look in the mirror and ask yourself, do the impulses come from the ELM tree and when it comes down to the decisions, don't listen to the little devil sitting on your left shoulder, instead take heed to the Angel sitting on the Right. Many people claim to be Religious God Loving and Fearing Christians but in reality, practice the religion of White Supremacy. We got to all fix our hearts. Love never Fails according to a pamphlet that a Jehovah's Witness left on my door recently.

I Love America But America Don't Love Me

I do love America! I'm a Volunteer Vietnam Era War time Veteran and took a chance on going to Vietnam for my country. My granddaughter is in boot camp as we speak, three out of 6 of my Mothers Brothers took the chance and her Baby Brother Joseph did go. His most painful memory that it took many years for the pain to subside, was his best friend a Mexican, Private First-Class Richard Corrales' from Texas dying in his arms. I have 2 friends since childhood, Oscar Tripplett whose brother Private First-Class A. W. Tripplett and Frank Vargas whose brother Private First-Class Marcelino Vargas Jr. also died in Vietnam.

I mentioned them for the second time to give Honor and say that many of us, our family and friends have made contributions with blood sweat and tears for the Love and Freedom of the United States of America. America, what will it take for you to Love us back? Can we wake up and face the errors and mistakes that we've made and Move On.

Fellow Americans, can we mend our hearts, fix our Moral Compasses and keep those with Anti-Christ and Demagogue Characteristics out of our lives and out of office. Can we focus on growing some ELM trees and be a part of America becoming an

161

even better place and be its' Greatest of All Time?" To some people, I know no matter what I or anybody else say, they're not going to Love anyway because of the evil that lurks within the hearts of those who practice and believe in White Supremacy and can't see the Forest for the trees. People can(should)(would) agree to disagree on some subjects but let's take Race out of it and practice eating the fruit from the ELM tree and applying ELMER in all our decisions.

In my case regarding some of the wrong against me, the simple truth of the matter beginning at an early age is that I didn't have to make the choices I made, but for lack of knowledge, guidance and understanding, racism and my own foolish Pride, I went down some wrong paths impeding progress to my success and on a path to call out America for these fouls against African Americans, others and to find ways to work on our Moral Principles as a Country.

It's going to be hard even though the 300 years that Willie Lynch spoke about on the banks of the James River passed in 2012 a lot of people Black and White still can't let go of that mentality.

Anyone who wants to see some good old southern justice in action, go visit the Forest Park Court especially, but any court while court is in session while court is in session if you are ever in the

Atlanta area. All you'll see is Just Us. The following letters are real

and examples of how I fought miscarriages of Justice and how you

can too. Remember that the paper trail works both directions:

****

████████████████

██████

July 10, 2017

Clayton County Internal Affairs
Unit Commander
Sergeant ██████████
9157 Tara Blvd
Jonesboro, GA 30293

Hello Sergeant ██████

How are you? Fine, I hope! My name is Eddie 'C' Byirt Jr. I am an ex- U. S. Marine, Disabled Vet, 31 Year retired U. S. Postal Service Letter Carrier and possess an AAS degree in Criminal Justice. I am writing to you because my search revealed no Internal Affairs Unit for the Forest Park, Georgia Police Department.

The need for this letter is that I believe that I'm a Repeat Victim of Racial Profiling by the Forest Park Police Department, in particular Officer ████████████████. The most recent incident occurred June 28th, 2017. I was stopped and issued a ticket "T Fail to Yield at Stop/Yield Sign. I followed another car slowly across the RR tracks looking left for approaching traffic the same as the person in front of me. After I was given the ticket, I went back to see how I could have missed a Stop Sign. There was a sign, but it was not where you would expect it to be in that it was further from the intersection than what is normal, and the large white stop line is before you reach the tracks. Also, if two people had to stop at the same time, the second car would most likely be sitting on the tracks. It is a trap and that is why ███████████ was hiding in the vicinity. My question to Officer ██████ is, "Why 'didn't you stop the person in front of me as well."

I had driven a pretty good distance from the crossing when I noticed ███████████████ behind me with blue lights on. I pulled over and was really surprised by ███████████████ politeness and demeanor and also his line of questions, such as "Where do you work, what's your phone number, do you still live at the same address on the license?" He was so nice and polite, that I thought I might get a warning. However, he came back with a ticket. That's when I noticed that there was a Clayton County Police behind ██████ ███████████ vehicle. I doubted that had I been a little old white lady or man would I have been stopped, let alone two cars for the stop.

The more I thought about what happened, I realized that ██████ ███████ was the same officer that had given me a bogus ticket previously. In that ticket he falsely accused me and testified against me in court. I was so disheartened by the miscarriage of Justice that I wrote the presiding Judge and she saw fit to bring me back to court to straighten out the false allegations made by ███████████ My fine was rescinded, but I still had to pay court costs. A copy of the letter to her is enclosed.

Lately I've experienced unusual activity on my phone, that I hadn't prior to giving ███████████████ my number that he wrote on a personal pad that didn't have anything to do with the issuance of the citation he wrote me on June 28th. I don't know for sure whether ███████████████ is responsible or not but, I am very leery due to his extra {even though fake} effort at being Kind and his unusual line of questioning. It is a proven fact that he has shown prejudice against me in the past. Three questions I'd like answered are, #1 why weren't the people that went across the tracks before me stopped, #2 why was 2 Police cars necessary to stop me and # 3 What does he need with my phone number? I feel in my heart that there are others with similar run-ins with ████████████ and shun the idea that his superiors have covered for him this long or are like minded in their thinking.

Sincerely,

Eddie C Byirt Jr.

Copy to:

Mayor ████████████
Forest Park, Georgia

(Mayor Pro-tem) ████████████

Interim City Manager/Chief
████████████

City Council Member
████████████

████████████

Atlanta, Georgia

165

January 4, 2011

The Honorable ████████
320 Cash Memorial Blvd.
Forest Park, GA 30297

Dear ██████████,

My name is Eddie "C" Byirt Jr. I'm a 5-year Marine Corps Veteran and 31 Year Letter Carrier for a total of 36 years retired in 11/09. I'm an honest law-abiding citizen and if I'm wrong I own up to it as I believe everybody should do.

I was in your court on 12-29-2010. I was fined $127.00 without being proved guilty. That was a miscarriage of justice because I'm not guilty. An appeal costs $205.00. If I had it, I would spend the $205.00 simply to prove my innocence. Enclosed you'll find this proof. I chose not to play the race card in court because you are Black and I thought the evidence would speak for itself, but you chose to go with the Officers prejudiced assumptions.

Like I told you in court, that was the very first day I drove that truck. I bought the truck on September 17th like I said knowing that it needed a transmission. I didn't know I had to put two mufflers on and pay another $200.00 to repair the frame. On the day I was stopped by Forest Park police, I'd finished my repairs and was on my way to get an emissions test that I knew was needed in order to get my tag. I didn't know that the seller ████████████████ was supposed to have done that prior to selling the Truck. Finally, after making all the repairs and passing the emissions test. I took the title and emissions to the Tag Office where I found that I couldn't get a tag with the title that I had listing me as the third party. The seller, ██████████ had failed to transfer the title into his name with the State and never applied for a tag. After finding that out, I had to go get ██████████, take him to the title office and pay out of my own pocket

166

for him to get the title in his name so that he could legally transfer title to me.

██████ who is white and lives in Forest Park drove the truck several months with that messed up "Tag Applied For" cardboard and was never stopped, but the very first day I drive it I'm pulled over? Look around your Court room Judge. What's really going on?

In late August, early September, Forest Park police stopped me in the 1978 Dodge Truck that I owned prior to buying the 1987 GMC truck, questioned me about the origin of my load, photographed me and issued a ticket for a seat belt violation, when everything else checked out. Up until that ticket I was unaware that the law had been changed regarding Seat Belts while riding in pickup trucks.

Racial Profiling was mentioned in two or three cases in your court on 12-29-2010. It is hard not considering that possibility when one walks into the Forest Park Courtroom seeking Justice and 90% of what you see is Just Us.

If honesty, integrity, fairness, justice and the willingness to do the right think means anything to you, hopefully, I'll hear from you before January 13, 2011. ██████, please don't be a willing supporter to the many miscarriages of Justice that I've witnessed each time I've been in Court in Forest Park, Georgia.

Sincerely,

Eddie "C" Byirt Jr.

****

I got my last ticket for being in a hurry. A Black female

turned it into an improper right turn. Details: As I approached an

intersection that I've travelled daily over twenty plus years, I saw that the person in the right lane had stopped way behind the white

line and was not proceeding to make the right turn which is legal at

that intersection and probably most worldwide. I saw the

opportunity to go around to the left and go past the cars sitting

behind the lady who didn't know the rules I went around without

speeding or causing a dangerous situation but before I could make

my turn, out of nowhere, she threw the blue lights on me, almost hit

my bumper and got on her loudspeaker ordering me to now go ahead

and make the right turn, but I couldn't because of the traffic now

flowing through the intersection. When I was finally able to make

the turn, I pulled over. upsetting traffic that had been flowing nicely.

For some reason or another, I thought of Barney Fife. It was

probably the loudspeaker. When she got to my car, I asked what

was the problem? She asked me if I was in a hurry, for my license

and went back to the Police car where she proceeded to interrupt the

flow of traffic somewhere in between 15 -30 minutes before she

came back with a ticket for, "Improper Right Turn", which I wasn't

able to complete until after she got behind me. I pointed that fact

out to her, and her reply was something to the effect of, "I'm not

going to argue with you Man, you can tell it to the Judge." So, the first time I went to court, I let the judge know that I wanted a jury trial. The second time I went, the DA assistant told me that the fine was only $50.00. To me that meant only $50.00 for them. After that, the insurance man wants his, at least $50.00 more but every month because 3 more points on your driving record. At print for this Book, I'm waiting on the outcome. I'd rather burn that $50. Up in gas fighting for fair. If the Law give her the Power to ad-lib like that, some citizens are already in trouble. Unfortunately, the Black Man is still low man on the totem pole and still facing an uphill battle. But we need our lady's support in certain areas. Some of you all are in the door, but please don't prop yourselves up riding our back with petty mess like this. Try ELMER.

Systematic Racism is still Super Bad civically and otherwise in Rockford, Illinois as well. On one occasion, I wasn't in the city 20 minutes when we got pulled over by Police traveling East on State Street, but made a U-turn to stop us when he saw us heading west on State and make a left on Johnson in a neighborhood that I spent time in when I lived there. The Police were surprised to see two old men as they approached with weapons already drawn. They told us that they didn't need probable cause to stop us because we were in a

Weed and Seed Area, something that I'd never heard of till that point. I was back in Atlanta a short time later when I heard that the Rockford Police had murdered an unarmed Black Man as he sought refuge in a church with a daycare and with many African American Children present. Just imagine the mental scarring that these children were left with. More recently I heard about a high school classmates' son Kerry Blake Jr. being murdered unarmed in his Grandmother's house while his Aunt and Uncle pleaded with officers outside to let them inside to defuse the situation.

In this day and time, there are some success stories but still far too many sad tales from the dark side. If I can lay the groundwork for just one young male to survive and succeed in the jungle of Racism, my book will not have been in vain.

If I can get just one racist who might be on the fence to come all the way over to the Love Side, then my book will not have been in vain. I have cousins on both sides who are bi-racial or in bi-racial relationships. Because of my past experiences, I admit that these relationships didn't sit well with me in the beginning but at the end of the day, it's the right thing to do and the only thing that should matter is that they Love each other.

I Love America But America Don't Love Me

Just look at some of the amazing results of some special love. We have some beautiful and amazing special people as a result of some of these colorblind relationships. Without this very special kind of Love there would not have been a President Barrack Obama, a Colin Kaepernick, a Fred VanVleet out of Rockford, IL, or like Atlanta DJ Greg Street say, "them light skin boys Steph Curry, and Clay Thompson from Golden State, Seth Curry, Patrick Mahomes II and Russell Wilson, the two starting quarterbacks in the 2019 Pro Bowl, Hines Ward, an Aaron Judges , a Devin Booker, a James Connor, a Carmelo Anthony, a Trey Young, a Cameron Heywood, a Phillip Lindsey, Tommy Pham, Rui Hachimura, a Hines Ward, a Tiger Woods, John Legend, Zack Levine, Drake or Atlanta's Frank Ski, or the golden goddesses Lena Horne, Eartha Kitt, Hailey Berry, Beyoncé, Alicia Keys, Rihanna, Meghan the Duchess of Sussex, Ashanti, Jasmine Guy, Tiny Harris and Mariah just to name a few as the list goes on and on. Indeed, the results of the love here is very special. Imagine how much further one would stick their chest out if one them was family. It's all about the Love. This is just a small part of what I believe Fred Hampton and Mark Clark before they was murdered as they slept, William "Preacher man" Fesperman,

I Love America But America Don't Love Me

Jack (June bug) Boykin, Bobbie Joe McGinnis and Hy Thurman of the Young Patriots Organization and Jose Cha-Cha Jiménez had in mind when they came up with the Rainbow Coalition and later Reverend Jesse Jackson when he launched the National Rainbow Coalition. These are but a few examples of mixed-race relationships that have brought Love and Happiness into millions of homes around the Globe and I feel America is a better place because of them and what they exemplify. They have all made me Proud.

Let's plant some EmpathyLoveMoral (ELM) trees, practice ELMER and be done with Racism, the Religion of White Supremacy and those practicing it. It has a different set of values and rules than those practiced by Bible Believing, God Fearing People and it violates our Pledge of Allegiance to the Flag of the United States of America!

SALUTES

First off, the Honorable President Barrack Obama, thanks for believing that "yes we could" and then doing it.

You did our country proud and America was in a better place.

Job well done! Thank you for your service.

SALUTES

American Businessman, Mr. Robert F. Smith, kudos to you for putting your money where your mouth is.

Thank you for your investment and emphasis on Education.

I've heard that with enough education, one can get anything in life that they desire if they apply themselves and stay focused.

Thank you, Sir, for your

contributions!

Salutes

Lebron James aka King James

Kudos to the King of Hoops for the school and for being outspoken for the right reasons even though he knows Republicans by tennis shoes too. Thanks for remaining true to your heart and acting.

Hands down the GOAT. If they ever put a picture for a definition of Basketball Player, it would be an injustice to not use the King.

There have been times when I wished he'd be a little selfish, then we could all have put the question about who the GOAT to rest.

Keep doing it King, you are doing it

well! Thank you for all that you do and did!

Salutes

I salute you Mr. Jalen Rose, for a nice NBA Career but mostly for the Jalen Rose Leadership Academy in Detroit Michigan. You saw the need and acted on it in a major way, realizing that "With enough education, one can get everything they want." Kudos to you!

Postscript

I had to pull my book offline one more time to add my take on the Coronavirus situation. As ugly as the real news and 45 himself is, I have to say it one more time "God don't like ugly". And there are too many Religious organizations and fake Christians serving the wrong Supreme Being.

Even though the Coronavirus hit all over the world, it hit no place harder than the United States of America. Thereby making America number 1 on his watch!

The way the U. S Constitution was abused by those in power in

I Love America But America Don't Love Me

the impeachment trial of 45 was a disgrace to the whole world.

America was supposed to be honorable, have integrity, be an example for the world to replicate and representative of Empathy, Love, Morals, Ethics, Respect! (ELMER). The GOP avoided any sniff of ELMER. Those that would sell their souls for gold, look where it brought us. If they didn't think that we could be brought to their knees, "Now you Know" in the words of Christopher Wallace.

I believe that God is the great equalizer and that that sham of a trial was large. For those fake Christians that still don't want to believe their lying eyes and stay on a sinking ship, I have a warning for you, Keep Playing!

I believe that America should represent Godly things and characteristics. Instead Lies, dishonesty, divisiveness and disorder became the rule and into effect on 45's inauguration day. That play with the Constitution was huge, therefore the acknowledgement had to be huge. It could be said that the Coronavirus, is the framers of the constitution turning over in their graves. I don't want to sound like a religious nut, but you better recognize. Man is not in control.

Remember the locusts and the plagues placed on Egypt because of a wicked pharaoh during biblical times. In the words of the

O'Jays, "Wake up Everybody". It's 2020, the year of perfect vision!

Practice ELMER but Love is the key to Peace and Harmony!

Made in USA - Kendallville, IN
1088937_9781702418133
04.23.2020 0814